MORE FLOWER ARRANGEMENT

The successor to *Flower Arrangement*, this book discusses flowers for almost every occasion—at home, in churches, for parties—and for all seasons of the year. There are also chapters on contemporary flower design, arrangements of fruit and flowers, pots-et-fleurs and dried materials. The author has included points on how to grow a number of the flowers he arranges, as well as interesting information about the origins of the names of and the legends attached to many of our everyday flowers. The book is profusely illustrated with drawings and plates, including four full-colour plates, and it aims to show how flowers, foliage, fruit and house plants can be arranged more effectively, efficiently and economically if the few well-proven principles of flower arrangement are followed. It will be of equal interest to the novice and the experienced flower arranger.

THE AUTHOR

Eric Roberts is a Past President of the Society of Floristry and a member of the International Panel of Judges of Floristry. He holds the Diploma of the Society of Floristry. His professional achievements include highest national awards for bridal floristry and sympathy flowers, the Royal Horticultural Society Silver Gilt Medals, Grenfell Medals and the Royal Welsh Horticultural Show Large Gold Medals.

TEACH YOURSELF BOOKS

MORE FLOWER ARRANGEMENT

Eric Roberts, S.F. (Dip.)

ST. PAUL'S HOUSE   WARWICK LANE
LONDON EC4P 4AH

First printed 1973

ISBN 0 340 16310 0

Printed in Great Britain for The English Universities Press Ltd
by Fletcher & Son Ltd, Norwich and bound by
Richard Clay (The Chaucer Press) Ltd, Bungay, Suffolk

Contents

List of Colour Plates

Acknowledgements

I would like to express my very sincere thanks to my staff and pupils who have helped and encouraged me in preparing this second book for the Teach Yourself series, particularly to Mrs. Marjorie Davies, Past President of the Cardiff Floral Decoration Society, and finally to my wife and daughter for their never failing patience and encouragement.

E.R.

Introduction—Flowers for Every Occasion

The beauty, form, colour and scent of flowers are among the most transient of things, yet their influence on our lives is greater than we care to admit. We arrive in the world more often than not to be greeted by flowers, we give or receive flowers throughout our lives, and I think most of us, if we are honest with ourselves, hope for a few at our departing. The language of flowers is much the same the world over, irrespective of colour, creed and climate. Flowers in window boxes grace (yes, that's the word) the exteriors of banks and other such austere institutions, and, what is more, they are to be found inside on the Board Room table as well as in the Private Secretary's office. In Post Offices and other Government buildings, we see little vases of flowers from the country or garden and the odd plant on a filing cabinet or office window sill. These are not at all within the laid-down establishment, but there they are—sometimes gay and fresh, sometimes looking a little sad and wilted, perhaps because there is a reluctance to throw away a memento of a happy occasion—a reminder of the beauty and tranquillity that can still be found in this noisy, hurrying, petrol-fume-laden society. These little nosegays are often arranged in a manner that is quite inspired, despite the fact that they may be in a jam jar, drinking glass or jug, and they spread their colour, beauty and, I like to think, influence for the good of us all.

Even in this efficient, computerised age, flowers and plants are increasingly more often officially approved and even specified. It has been proved that in the modern open-planned offices not only do staff prefer to work in sections defined by groups of plants instead of by portable partitions but they are also actually more efficient. These arrangements, however, are installed and arranged by specialists, and consequently are both decorative and functional.

The object of this book is to show how flowers, fruit and house plants can be arranged more effectively, efficiently and economically if the few well-proven basic principles of flower arrangement are followed, and how anyone who is sufficiently interested can produce more and still better flower arrangements for every occasion.

Part 1—Techniques and Technicalities

1 Basic Principles of Flower Arrangement

Design, *proportion*, *balance* and *harmony*—these are the four fundamental principles of any art form, although today there are some schools of thought that seem anything but harmonious. However, we will not argue that point, so let us examine these principles as they apply to flower arrangements for all occasions.

Design, *proportion*, *balance* and *harmony*—lovely words, and they conjure up visions of lovely things: of flowers in arrangements for churches, weddings, christenings, parties, Golden and Silver Wedding anniversaries, the Harvest Festival, Christmas and Easter. All the year round there are flowers to be arranged, and what could be more encouraging than the knowledge that an understanding of these four basic principles will enable us to express ourselves in a far more pleasant way than we had ever imagined possible.

We all have our moments when we are inspired and everything goes right, but unfortunately there is the other side of the coin when nothing does. We plan, we prepare and then, for no apparent reason, everything seems impossible. This is too short, we haven't enough of that, and that clashes with this! And so on and so forth—our confidence ebbs away and we are near to despair. Sometimes we are fortunate and someone is at hand to give us expert guidance. Why is it that some people can do this? It is because they have studied and mastered the technicalities—the four basic principles and the five ancillaries that make up the *nine* essentials in the technique of flower arranging.

They may not always feel inspired, but their study has ensured a disciplined approach to the problem, and while the result may not always be a masterpiece, it will conform to the basic principles and thus be acceptable anywhere.

These basic principles have been discussed in considerable detail in *Flower Arrangement* (Teach Yourself Books). Even so, I think they can be repeated again and again with equal benefit to the beginner and the expert. When something 'just doesn't go right' it is generally because we have forgotten or misapplied one or other of the basic rules.

This simple chart is how I keep them in my mind.

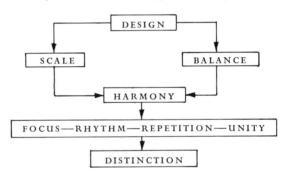

Design

You will see that I have put this at the head of my chart. This is because it is the pattern on which the whole arrangement depends—its shape, height, width and depth. A design does not just happen; it is the result of a well-thought-out plan. The selection of flowers, foliage and container for an arrangement must always be made with an idea of how and where they will be used.

As with almost everything that is worth while, practice is

essential and therefore a certain amount of drudgery must be faced. But don't let this prospect put you off, because the joy and satisfaction you will gain every time you achieve a better flower arrangement will make it all worth while. Furthermore, you will have opened up to yourself a field of self-expression that you had never believed possible.

You must always have the ultimate shape of your arrangement in your mind's eye, and therefore I feel it is a good thing to think at first in terms of *form*, not of colour. The silhouette should be clear and pleasing. A good design should be three-dimensional, with transition between the various 'parts'. None of the mechanics should be visible, and the back of a design is, in its way, as important as the front, on which it can have no little influence.

Scale or Proportion

This applies to the size relationship of the various component parts of an arrangement as well as to that of the finished arrangement to its surroundings. It is the relationship of the flowers, foliage, container and accessories one to the other, and their relationship to the furnishings, décor and size—and general 'atmosphere'—of the room or location in which they are to be placed. For instance, a medium-sized arrangement of small flowers will be lost in the middle of a church, whereas it will be completely right and in proportion if placed on a window sill or a small altar. Likewise, a large arrangement of chrysanthemum blooms or sunflowers in an urn will be overpowering in a normal-sized sitting room but could look quite right in the average entrance hall. As with so many things, the functional aspect is important and, providing the technique is correct, if an arrangement looks right, it generally is right.

Balance or Stability

This is both actual and visual, though as far as flower arrangements are concerned it is largely visual. Balance is dependent on anchorage and the even distribution of size, weight and colour. For instance, dark colours appear heavier than light ones. Texture also influences balance. Rough surfaces absorb light; smooth and shiny surfaces reflect light, and influence colour harmonies. Objects can appear larger than they actually are. Balance may be symmetrical or asymmetrical.

Harmony

This is very difficult to define because it is largely aesthetic. Colours and textures, sizes and shapes are pleasing in harmony. Lack of scale or proportion and awkward or square shapes generally create discord. Harmony is a oneness of spirit, mood, theme and purpose that completes 'the picture'. It is an agreement of artistic effects, forming a concordant whole.

Focus or Focal Area

This is the area or point to which the eye is drawn and from which it radiates outwards over the whole design. It is the point from which all stems should seem to originate, or where they meet or cross, as is the tying-point in a bunch of flowers where all the stems are secured; the place to which they converge and from which they emerge. It is very closely related to balance, harmony and accent. Think for a moment how these 'parts' are affected by focus. A focal point that is in the wrong place can destroy rhythm; it can put a composition completely out of balance. It can turn something quiet, pleasing and harmonious or exciting and dramatic into a conglomeration of rank bad taste or even vulgarity.

Focus or focal point can be obtained by the use of a single flower or a number of flowers, by the use of a contrasting colour, or even by a different shape or texture. Ribbon or the judicious placing of an ornament or some accessory can be used to create a focal point. A gift, such as a bottle of scent or wine, or a piece of jewellery, if correctly placed will produce a satisfactory, pleasing and practical focal point. Very occasionally, a genius will produce a design whose focal point is a void—a space. We can see instances of this in some of the flower paintings by the Dutch Masters.

Rhythm or Visual Movement

This is flow or swing from the focal point, the 'tying point' or the centre of gravity. Rhythm is obtained by continuity of *line*, by the balancing and counter-balancing of curves and other shapes.

This is the first occasion that I have mentioned *line*. In flower arrangement it is inseparable from rhythm. My *Oxford Dictionary* lists a very large number of definitions for line. One I like very much is 'line of beauty with two opposite curves, like an elongated S'. Surely this must mean 'the Hogarth curve' or 'lazy S', that languorous, serpentine, graceful, rhythmic flow, the very embodiment of continuous movement. There are, of course, other lines: vertical, horizontal, crescent, pyramid, triangular, circle and oval. There is no square line!

Continuity or Repetition

Very closely related to accent and rhythm, this is the repeating of items of colour or form. It greatly helps the blending of colour and shapes, and prevents hard and fast unrhythmic divisions.

Unity

Unity is the general 'tying up' of the whole design: the arrangement of the flowers with the container, and these with the background and the position in which the design is to be displayed.

Distinction

This could be called emphasis or accent. It involves giving some particular part of an arrangement prominence or making it more conspicuous than another part. Although I suppose allied to it, it must not be confused with the focal point, which must be related to the whole. Distinction is really that indefinable something which lifts an arrangement out of the ordinary. It is called 'cut' by tailors, but I prefer to call it inspiration. I hope that there will be many moments when you will be inspired.

2 Colour

Colour awareness: some have it, others have not. Countless books have been written on this vast subject, and no doubt will continue to be written, and while I do not think a deep and concentrated study of the subject is absolutely necessary to the flower arranger I do think a basic understanding of it is essential. It is said that colour adds a fourth dimension to design. In any case, it is an exciting subject, and one that we can play with and enjoy.

There are many useful books and pamphlets available to those who wish to make a study of colour. The Royal Horticultural Society and the Society of Floristry both issue booklets on this subject, and it has been discussed in considerable detail in *Flower Arrangement* (Teach Yourself Books). I will therefore only touch on it briefly here.

Reduced to its simplest form, I think colour in flower arrangements can best be understood and applied by, so to speak, dividing the spectrum in half. Using true red as a centre or base, we have the yellows and yellow-reds becoming orange on the one side, and the blues and blue-reds becoming violet on the other. The hues, tints and shades of one set of colours tend to give you *warmth* and are generally better used in artificial or poor light; those of the other set tend towards *coolness* and are generally more suitable in situations where the light is good. I am not considering fluorescent lighting, which completely distorts some colours and for which special allowance must be made for each separate occasion. Very broadly speaking, mixing the two sets of colours produces your *colour harmonies*, complementary or analogous, etc.

Lighting has a very considerable effect on colour and colour harmonies. The brighter the light, the more dramatic and intense the colours appear. They are naturally nearer to pure hues in a good light. Subdued lighting is generally more harmonious and restful, and mistakes or imperfections are not so apparent. I will not go further than this at this juncture because to me colour awareness, like beauty, is in the eye of the beholder—witness some of the present-day psychedelic (not a pretty word) fabrics in clashes of colour hitherto undreamed of that have produced many very exciting displays, *but*, I submit, only because at least one of the *basic principles* of design was there, i.e. *proportion*.

3 Aids—the Mechanics of Flower Arrangement

The 'mechanics' of Occidental flower arrangement are of comparatively recent origin. They are also relatively simple but of the utmost importance. Without them there can be little certainty that an arrangement on which much time and thought has been spent will remain in anything like the shape or form intended.

A good anchorage is the fundamental base from which all arrangements should start. This, of course, is of particular importance when an arrangement is intended for exhibition and may have to be transported in a finished or semi-finished state to the place of the show. There is nothing more infuriating than, after having spent a lot of time and thought on an arrangement, to find that it collapses if the table on which it is standing is knocked. In my experience it is practically impossible to rearrange it as it was before. You must start right. Not only must the Oasis block, pin-holder, wire netting or polystyrene, etc., provide a suitable anchorage for every piece of foliage and flower stem but also it must itself be securely anchored to the container. Oasis Fix, plasticene, Oasis adhesive tape and soft florists' wire are the products most generally used to ensure good anchorage to the container. No description of these products and the 'aids' with which they are used is necessary because with most of the arrangements illustrated in this book there is a small sketch showing the 'mechanics'. They have, in any case, been discussed at some length in *Flower Arrangement* (Teach Yourself Books).

All these aids to the 'mechanics' of flower arrangement are obtainable from any good florist, who will gladly explain or demonstrate their uses. They are shown in illustrations nos. 1 and 2.

One word of warning. Be sure that your container—vase, bowl, dish or whatever it is—is quite clean and dry— particularly that it is dry—before fixing your mechanics. Also, while doing this preparation work, make sure that you have left a convenient place for filling the container with water.

Key: 1 Oasis brick $9 \times 4\frac{1}{2} \times 4\frac{1}{2}$ inches
   2 Oasis Fix
   3 Plastic-covered 2-inch mesh wire netting
   4 Oasis round
   5 Oasis square
   6 Oasis round in glazed pottery urn
   7 Oasis round in urn vase covered with 2-inch mesh wire netting strapped with Oasis tape
   8 Gutter Percha tape—green, white and brown
   9 Multi-cut scissors
  10 Small pruning knife
  11 Pinholders—round $1\frac{1}{2}$–3 inches diameter; rectangular up to $1\frac{1}{2} \times 4$ inches
  12 Polystyrene sheet—green or white
  13 Polystyrene rounds
  14 Polystyrene squares and rectangles, showing adhesive pads
  15 Wire cutters
  16 Plasticine
  17 Florapak

Note: Nos. 13 and 14 are supplied with adhesive pads.

I   AIDS AND ACCESSORIES

2   AIDS AND ACCESSORIES

Key : 1 Pinholder secured in glass goblet with Oasis Fix
     2 Candle cup secured in candlestick with Oasis Fix
     3 Pinholder with hole for candle secured in candle cup with
       Oasis Fix
     4 Specially-made Oasis bowl with Oasis round
     5 Oasis frog
     6 Large pinholder secured in pan with Oasis Fix

4 The Suitability of Containers

The suitability or otherwise of a container for an arrangement of flowers is very much a matter of opinion. One person will think flowers in a teapot perfectly charming, while another will think the very idea quite shocking. Some prefer pewter, brass or copper, while others delight in fine porcelain or glass, and then there are those who think rough, unglazed, hand-thrown pottery the only suitable container for flowers. It is how and where you use your container that really matters, and here a few basic rules must be observed.

Obviously the first thing to ascertain is whether the container you propose to use will hold water. If not, is it possible to make it watertight? There are countless ways in which this can be done and we shall discuss a few later. The second thing to be sure of is will the container stand firmly when filled with water and holding flowers? Finally, you must ask yourself whether the container will be in harmony with the flowers you intend to use, and will the two together be in harmony with their surroundings? This last point is, to my mind, the most important and, strange to say, the most often ignored.

Containers that can hold sufficient water and support suitable holders and other forms of flower 'mechanics' but are otherwise unsuitable or unsightly can be used if hidden by driftwood, stones, moss or shells. The mechanics in shallow bowls can also be hidden in this manner.

Some containers, while being completely watertight, will mark a polished or delicate surface through condensation.

Bowls or vases with concave bases are particular offenders, so be sure to place them on a mat.

Glass ware—particularly goblets, brandy balloons and, though not quite so obvious, gold-fish bowls—has a number of different uses as flower containers. The mechanics required vary from the very simple to the quite complicated, but all are effective. The traditional glass trumpet flower vase is, in my opinion, one of the best containers for such delicate garden flowers as sweet peas, roses, pinks and border carnations. Little, if any, mechanics are required with this vase to hold these flowers in their required positions.

A Word about Baskets

Baskets vary in design, shape, size and colour as much as almost any other household article one can think of, yet almost every one can be used as a container for flower arrangements. From the practical Sussex trug (the most useful kind of gardening basket I know) to the delicate open basket weave of Beleek, Dresden and other rare porcelains, the variety is infinite, and so are the ways of using baskets for flower arrangements.

First, I think we should remember that a basket was originally an article of everyday and household use. It was intended as something in which things could be conveniently carried, or by which they could be lifted and transported from one place to another. Therefore, baskets had handles of some sort or another. To my mind there is little point in using a basket for flower decoration if its chief characteristic, its handle, is not visible and usable. A baking tin, any old pot or bucket might just as well be used, provided that it does, or can be made to, hold water. So, if a basket has a handle (some have two or more), it should be clearly visible and, if possible, usable as well. Don't let us, however, become confused with basket ware—articles in basket weave. We are dealing here with containers that were originally designed to make the carrying of things easier. So I repeat—don't forget the handle. It has got to be part of your design. In certain circumstances, the handle can even provide your focal point.

Generally speaking, the basic design pattern for flower arrangements in baskets is either horizontal or vertical; therefore, it will readily be appreciated that balance, particularly visual balance, is of the utmost importance. In my opinion, line arrangements seldom, if ever, look well in baskets.

A basket such as a Sussex trug (see drawings nos. 3 and 4) calls for an arrangement that is horizontal and informal. It also requires the right setting—a hall table or the chancel steps at Harvest Festival immediately spring to mind.

The arrangement shown in drawing no. 3 has very few faults from the technical point of view. To my mind, however, it is quite unsuitable for its container. It is utterly impractical, would be difficult to pick up and looks as though it would easily overbalance, despite the fact that there is very little wrong with it in composition. Such an arrangement would look well in a copper pan or soup tureen. Or, if a basket must be used (some churches have these as part of their equipment), it should be a Gainsborough or similar type of tall basket, as shown in drawing no. 5. It will be noted that no alteration has been made to the placement or positioning of any flower and yet the arrangement looks quite stable, although the tallest gladiolus leans backwards. One of the others does, however, lean forwards sufficient to provide a counterbalance. Looked

Trug lined with plastic sheet
Oasis brick wire-netting wrapped

3   Basket arrangement—*wrong*

4 Basket arrangement—right

at from the purist's point of view, there should be another gladiolus pointing left and slightly downwards.

5   Another correct basket arrangement

Baskets that will not hold water can be satisfactorily adapted in a variety of ways. Bowls or tins can often be found that will fit inside and hold Florapak or Oasis, or simply crumpled wire netting. If these are not available, a basket that is not watertight or has an interior that must be protected can be lined with plastic sheet, pleated neatly to the inside shape and then cut round to just below the edge of the basket. The shape of such a plastic container can be made permanent for re-use by pinning or stapling the folds. Sellotape can also be stuck on the outside of the plastic to preserve the desired shape.

5 Placement

This is probably the most important part of flower arranging. It has an influence on almost every aspect of the design. I say design because I feel strongly that any flower arrangement, if it is to satisfy, must have a basis of design. This may be unobtrusive and subtle, even accidental. But it is very rarely that flowers just 'plonked' into a container produce a completely satisfactory effect. Almost always there is some rearrangement to be done. A pull here or a push there, shortening a stem or two, or removing an unwanted leaf— just like the final patting of the hair after brushing or combing. However, unlike the hair, flowers lose their natural anchorage once they are cut and have somehow to be fixed. We have to provide some means of support, and it is the way in which we use the various means of support that controls the whole design. We have to provide a point of origin from which all stems must seem to emerge. In a plant or a tree this is the point where the stem or trunk joins the root, and although a cut flower or foliage stem may in actual fact be quite remote from that point it must appear to emerge directly from it. If this principle is not strictly adhered to, no really satisfactory result is possible.

Sometimes it is possible to get away with a stem that does not come directly from the point of origin by using foliage or some other material to conceal that particular part of the stem. It must, however, be remembered that this extra use of foliage or other materials may give the whole arrangement a heavier appearance at the base than is intended or required.

Also, unless anchorage is completely secure, the part of the stem that is meant to show may swing either way and thus upset the rhythm of the whole arrangement. This swing—actual movement, as distinct from visual movement—matters not at all, provided that the anchorage is secure. A well-placed unit should always have the suggestion of movement or rhythm.

The point of origin need not necessarily be in the middle of a container. It is usually so with vases, jugs and tubs, or any container whose height is more than or equal to its width. Bowls, pans and some contemporary pottery dishes, however, lend themselves to a point of origin that is offset, not central; but here great care must be taken not to upset the balance, remembering, of course, that balance can be symmetrical and asymmetrical.

This single point of origin does not apply to planted arrangements. These are of composite construction, and each unit in the composition has its own individual point of origin.

The point or area of origin, while being very closely related to the focal point, must not be confused with it.

Colour blending is naturally a matter of personal preference, but even in this placement is important. There must be a transition of one colour, tone or shade with another. And weight of colour must, of course, be considered, otherwise visual balance will be upset.

Odd or even numbers of flowers? Personally, I don't think it matters very much. The success of an arrangement depends on its design and the correct placement of the flowers and foliage. Given the right container and the necessary minimum of suitable foliage, an arrangement of any number of flowers from one upwards is therefore possible, and if the arrangement conforms to all the basic principles

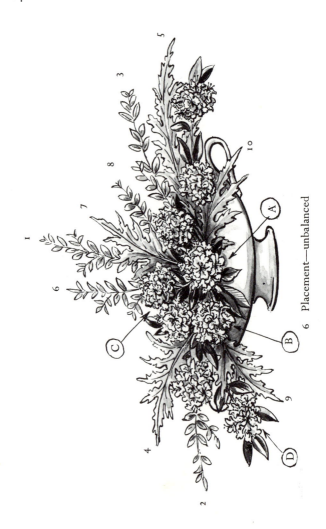

6 Placement—unbalanced

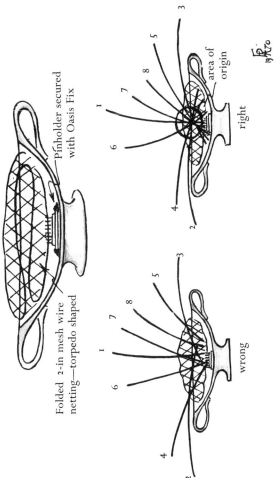

Folded 2-in mesh wire netting—torpedo shaped

Pinholder secured with Oasis Fix

area of origin

right

wrong

6A   Placement—the mechanics and how the area of origin is achieved

of design it will please most people. This question of numbers is discussed further in the next chapter.

The arrangement shown in drawing no. 6 of nine rhododendron flowers, five artichoke leaves and five sprays of cornus or privet illustrates an example of the incorrect placement of odd numbers. Actually, it is only the misplacement of *one flower* and *one piece of foliage* that has completely upset the whole composition.

First, you will notice that there appears to be a slight tilting effect to the left. This can be rectified by moving the head of flower unit C over to the right, thus restoring balance but leaving an empty space just above flower unit A. The most glaring fault, however, is that there appear to be two focal points. Rhododendron flowers A and B seem to be fighting each other for prominence. Our eye moves from one to the other and then, because of the tilting effect, over to the left, instead of being directed to flower A and from there radiating over the whole arrangement.

The cause of this appearance of two focal points is the misplacement of one piece of foliage, that is artichoke no. 4. You will see that this points directly in an arrow-like manner to rhododendron flower B. In other words, it has a different point of origin from all the other units that make up the whole arrangement.

Drawing no. 7 shows a partial correction. The repositioning of artichoke leaf no. 4, now stemming from and leading the eye to the area of origin, has placed an emphasis on rhododendron flower head A, flower head B immediately assuming much less importance. Unfortunately, however, the whole arrangement still appears to tilt to the left.

I did not want to do the whole arrangement again, but after some thought I felt it would be quicker in the long run to do so. Drawing no. 8 shows the final result. I have

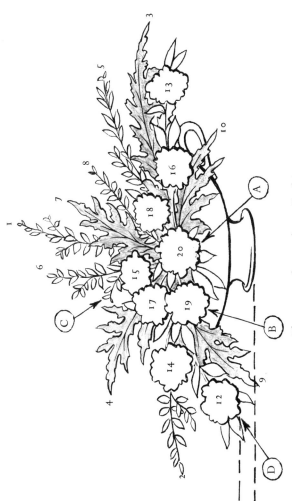

7 Placement—better, but still tilting

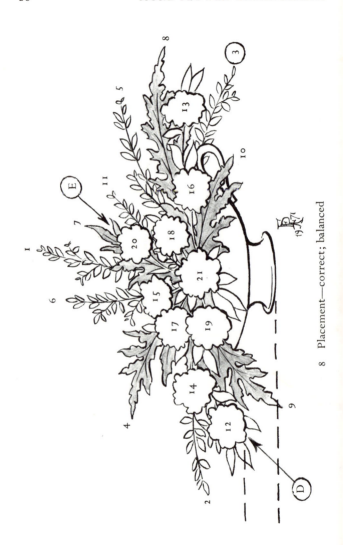

8 Placement—correct; balanced

numbered each flower and foliage unit in its order of placement.

   You will notice that these numbers start with the
extremities—i.e. we must first establish the height and
width of our arrangement to give us our scale or proportion.
I then work from side to side, thus ensuring balance of
weight and, at the same time, aiding the transition of
different colours or textures. While I always keep the position of the focal point in mind, I don't think it matters
much if it is placed early or late. In this particular case it
was the last unit to be placed, but I had taken the precaution
of selecting the best rhododendron flower head before I
started arranging.

   To really satisfy myself I felt an extra rhododendron
flower head (E) and one extra piece of cornus or privet
(no. 3) was necessary. The extra flower head added height,
which improved the proportions, and the extra piece of
foliage improved the balance. Also, by raising rhododendron
flower head D, the tilting effect was eliminated without any
loss of rhythm.

6 Odds or Evens?

'Always use odd numbers!' 3, 5, 7 and 9 are the mystical numbers that seem to govern the work of a large number of flower arrangers to such an extent that to many it has become an inflexible rule—I wonder why. Is it because two flowers seem incomplete and that four will inevitably result in a square or rectangle—shapes that have no line or rhythm?

As I have already said, I don't think it matters much how many or how few flowers you use, whether odd or even numbers. It is all a question of composition, of achieving balance and harmony with the other components that go to make up an arrangement, which can be foliage, branches or all kinds of other things.

Arrangements by some of the Japanese masters—Mr. Yuchiku Fujiwara and Mr. Teshigawara Wafu are but two—which are the very embodiment of line and rhythm, are often composed of two flowers and two branches, or sometimes four flowers. Even numbers! Four units! However, I think we should remember that Ikebana (and there are different schools of thought in this) has its own very rigid rules. These rules are born of age-old religious thought and custom, and necessitate much contemplation and selection—all too time-consuming for the average Occidental who 'does the flowers'.

The Japanese are becoming more and more interested in Western ways, and particularly in European and American flower arrangement. With their growing industrial success, much that was traditional to their way of life and behaviour has been relegated to the ceremonious occasion.

As an average Englishman, I have always associated Japan with a rather leisurely way of life. Large in my imagination loomed Mount Fugi, cherry blossom and Japanese gardens, geishas, Ikebana, the kimono and the Tea Ceremony. Much of this has now gone. The young Japanese today do not have time for these traditional activities. For instance, the kimono with its 'obi' and all the complicated lacing takes twenty to twenty-five minutes to be fixed to the satisfaction of the discriminating Japanese.

By the same token, traditional Ikebana as we understand it (for the word really means 'flower arrangement') takes too long. There just is not the time for the necessary contemplation and selection of the perfect flower or branch for the particular mood in mind. Chairs have largely taken the place of mats, and the Japanese, now very much apartment dwellers, seem to have little, if any, room for the *butzudan* or household shrine. Everything must now be geared to the demands of a highly successful industrial state. Small wonder, then, that the simpler to do and less time-consuming ways of obtaining aesthetic satisfaction are being sought.

We, too, are having changes forced on us. Standardisation and computerisation, and the consequent reduction in the variety of choice, are having their effect on Occidental flower arrangement. Simpler and more stylised arrangements seem to be becoming more popular, many of which have a distinctly Oriental flavour.

This somewhat lengthy discourse is intended to emphasise that, providing the principles of design are present and one has gained the necessary manual dexterity, many rules can be bent or even discarded. It also brings home to one the value of a garden, or even a window box or a few pot plants, which, with a little forethought, can provide some of the variety so difficult to buy these days.

To return to the question of numbers. In the following five chapters I discuss ways of achieving simple and attractive arrangements using one, two, three, four, five and ten flower units—odd and even numbers.

7 Single-flower Arrangements

Not only can a single-flower arrangement be quick and easy to do but also in the correct place, such as on a desk, mantelpiece or dressing table, it will often be much more effective than any other kind of arrangement.

In spring and early summer, magnolia, rhododendron and roses are followed as the year advances by paeonies, more roses, then dahlias and finally chrysanthemums. These are some of the large blooms that lend themselves to arrangements in a small goblet or champagne glass.

A perfect single bloom in the right setting is quite jewel-like, but, as with all good jewellery, the setting is of the utmost importance. The correct use of the foliage (as well as the container) will provide this. And, what is more, if the foliage is properly arranged—and separately—it will last two or three changes of flower. To my mind there is little more beautiful than a full-blown rose. Twice a year, for about ten days at a time, these are in abundance, so why not use them?

Drawing no. 9 shows one of various ways of preparing a base setting for a single flower, in this case a large rose (imagine 'Peace' or 'Crimson Glory') in a champagne glass. At first you may have to search a little among your rose bushes for just the right leaves, but as you become more practised you will see how many there are that have just the right curve or are exactly the right shape and size.

The simplest way of making a one-flower arrangement is, of course, merely to place the bloom in the goblet and

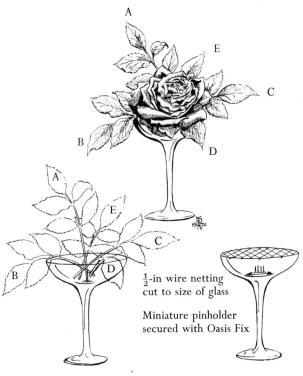

½-in wire netting
cut to size of glass

Miniature pinholder
secured with Oasis Fix

9   A single rose in a champagne glass

arrange the foliage around it. The great disadvantages of this
are that it is not very secure, 'line' is somewhat restricted
and you have to re-do the foliage every time a flower is re-
newed. The smallest pinholder and some fine mesh wire are,
in my opinion, the essential 'mechanics'. Single-flower
arrangements are equally attractive inside clear-glass brandy
balloons, in bowls and in specimen vases.

10   A single rose in a Venetian glass decanter

A single rose in a specimen vase or a decanter is a beautiful thing. In June or July—in fact, all the time that roses are
in bloom—you will see on your bushes one or more roses
on a long stem with foliage that is quite perfectly spaced.
Cut the stem as long as you can. It will not harm your rose
bush—in fact, quite the reverse: it will benefit from this
'summer pruning'. Don't worry should a caterpillar or an
earwig have eaten a hole or two in the odd leaf if the form
and texture of the rose are otherwise perfect. Drawing
no. 10 is of a single rose picked from my garden and placed
in a green Venetian glass decanter. No support of any sort
was necessary. The glossy green leaves toned perfectly with
the clear and coloured glass. The ravages of some insect or
other did not seem to matter at all.

8 Two-flower Arrangements

Two flowers are not the easiest of numbers to arrange. In fact, to many people they are the most difficult. Now, with decimalisation and our bunches of flowers in fives and tens instead of sixes and dozens, two arrangements from one bunch of tulips, daffodils or iris seem virtually impossible. Actually, it is not quite as bad as all that. We can still have two arrangements—three flowers in one and two in another —from one bunch if we use a little ingenuity.

Drawing no. 11 shows an arrangement of two tulips. From my store of dried materials, grasses, preserved foliages, etc. (every flower arranger should have such a store), I have taken two pencil bulrushes. These can be used time and again if about 6 inches of the bottom of the stem are taped and varnished to prevent rotting. The heads should also be varnished to stop seeding. These bulrushes have been stuck firmly into a $1\frac{1}{2}$-inch pinholder securely fixed to the bottom of the bowl with Oasis Fix centrally or offset as you fancy. The longer of your two tulips is placed immediately in front of the bulrushes. Carefully remove the bottom leaf from the second tulip, reduce it to about two-thirds the length of the other one and position it immediately in front of the other, leaning slightly forwards right. The leaf you have removed is then placed opposite this tulip. The large beach pebbles are now placed carefully round the pinholder. Make sure when doing this that the point where the two front pebbles meet is directly in front of the longest tulip stem. This join or meeting place constitutes your focal point.

11   Two tulips arranged in a shallow bowl with two bulrushes;
     the mechanics are concealed by pebbles

A more obvious focal point could, of course, be achieved by adding another furled or coiled leaf. You could also use an entirely different flower—or a bunch of violets or snow-drops, though if you do this you will not have a *two-flower* arrangement.

To my mind two roses make one of the nicest two-flower arrangements, but then the rose is my favourite flower. I don't know who named it the 'Queen of Flowers', but to me it is just that. I never cease to marvel at the in-built beauty of this flower: the scroll-like curves of the petals and their texture, which in some varieties, such as 'Crimson Glory' or 'Etoile de Hollande', rivals finest velvet. And, in addition, a fragrance that is quite unique. All this is available to the smallest gardener from June to the autumn. Cut in coloured bud and properly conditioned, a rose will develop to its full in water, lasting for anything from three to six days.

This does not mean to say that an arrangement of roses can just happen. To get the best out of your roses you should have your arrangement planned in your mind. Look at them carefully before cutting. Imagine this or that one in the vase you have in mind. If its foliage does not match the quality of the bloom, look for a suitable piece somewhere else on the bush—or even on another—and, bearing in mind the subse-quent shape of the bush, cut to just above an outward-facing bud.

The two roses in the rather elegant bottle-shaped vase (see drawing no. 12) are an example of an unplanned arrange-ment which does little to enhance the beauty of either the vase or the flowers. It is pedestrian, unexciting; it lacks rhythm. It is, in fact, 'just two roses in a vase'. A specimen vase with a heavy base would seem to be a much more suit-able container. However, a little more than merely a change

12   Unplanned arrangement of two roses

of vase is necessary; a few more buds and some extra foliage
are required. But we are still left with the problem of the
shortness of the stems of the two roses, which were cut to
about 4 inches and 8 inches respectively. As it happens, we
can with no great difficulty lengthen these stems (see drawing no. 13). Any suitable stem will do, bound onto the
main stem with cotton, soft wire or even Sellotape. With

13   Planned arrangement of two roses not entirely suited to the
     container

14   Silhouette drawing showing two containers to which this
     arrangement of two roses is better suited

the addition of extra buds and foliage, a much better arrangement of two roses results.

Now, imagine this arrangement in the little bottle-shaped vase (see drawing no. 14). I have shown it in silhouette form because this is the best way to picture—in your mind's eye— the subsequent shape of your arrangement. At this stage of an arrangement colour can be confusing or, at any rate, influence one to the detriment of form or line and rhythm. The whole arrangement is better suited to this vase, but I think it is still top heavy. A more bulbous or Persian-style vase, which is shown in dotted outline in drawing no. 14, is surely the most suitable.

Two full-blown roses on a plate or floating in a glass bowl make a delightful table-centre, as do two bosses of hydrangea flowers with their own foliage or another, such as *Bergenia cordifolia*. The possibilities are endless if you think about it.

Economy—Two Gladioli

The origin of the gladiolus—the sword lily—goes back thousands of years, probably to the Middle East, although the species we know today mostly come from South Africa. The gladiolus has an infinite range of colour, from pastel pink to royal purple and from primrose-yellow to brilliant scarlet and flame, and it varies in size from giant to miniature. The flowers, which can have frilled or plain edges, gradually open to the topmost bud.

Gladioli are available at the florist all the year round. They are a very economical flower, considering their long life as a cut flower and the fact that they are equally suitable for arrangements in a small sitting room or a cathedral, and thus are a good buy even in midwinter, when they are imported by air.

Planted in the smallest suburban garden with a little planning, gladioli can be available for cutting from June to September. They should be picked when the lowest bud is

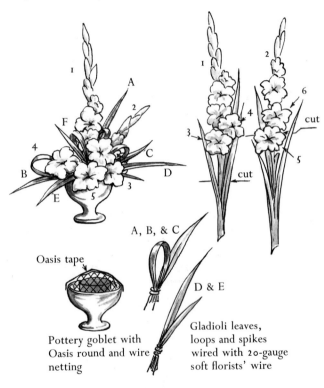

Oasis tape

Pottery goblet with
Oasis round and wire
netting

A, B, & C

D & E

Gladioli leaves,
loops and spikes
wired with 20-gauge
soft florists' wire

15   Economy arrangement using just two gladioli spikes

just opening. If you wish to save the corms for another year, be careful not to cut too much foliage. Allow the plant to die back, lift and dry under cover for protection from frost.

Two large gladioli may seem awkward subjects for a medium-sized arrangement in a pottery grapefruit bowl. However, it is quite easy to achieve if you follow the numbers and directions of drawing no. 15.

No. 1 gladiolus is cut as shown to about four times the height of the goblet. Take care not to damage the foliage when cutting the stem—every leaf is needed. Carefully remove flowers nos. 3 and 4, leaving each with as much of its own little stem as possible. Cut no. 2 gladiolus to about two-thirds the length of no. 1 and carefully remove flower no. 6.

Place no. 1 gladiolus in a vertical position one-third from the back of the goblet. No. 2 gladiolus is then positioned at an angle of about 45°, leaning slightly right and forward. The detached flowers nos. 3 and 4 are then placed as shown, followed by loops A, B and C, loop A leaning slightly back. Now add spikes D and E, spike E pointing slightly forward. The focal flower no. 5, which is attached to the remaining part of the main stem, is then reduced to the required length and positioned as shown. Loop F is added above this, pointing slightly forward. No. 6 detached flower placed behind gladiolus spike no. 1 completes the arrangement of *two* gladioli.

It could be argued that this is a five- or six-flower arrangement, as four blooms or florets have been detached from the two main flower spikes. However, since the gladioli bud spikes are so prominent, I think I shall stick to my opinion that it is a *two-flower* arrangement.

9 Three-flower Arrangements

Three Zinnias

This brilliant, long-lasting flower, which was introduced into this country from Mexico in the late eighteenth century, should surely be given a place in the small garden. Zinnias have a quality of brightness and jewel-like colourings that make them invaluable for mixed arrangements, particularly in late summer and early autumn.

On their own, they may at first sight seem very difficult to arrange because of their stiff, somewhat unrhythmic stems, so unlike the graceful curves of the gerbera (Barbiton daisy), the only other flower that, to my mind, has such a variety of pure dramatic colour.

Another disadvantage is their soft, hollow stems below the bloom down to the first leaf joint. If they are not properly conditioned before arranging, they may flop because of the weight of the bloom. There are, however, two simple ways of overcoming this problem. One is to wrap them in newspaper, as one would to straighten tulips, and leave them in deep water for a few hours. Another, and quicker, method is to 'wire' support the bloom. A 20-gauge soft florists' wire is simply pushed into the centre of the bloom down *inside* the hollow stem until the resistance of the first leaf joint is encountered; the surplus wire is then cut off. I can assure you that there will not be any diminution in the natural lasting qualities of the flower or its foliage. Many florists will have done this before sale, or will do so on request.

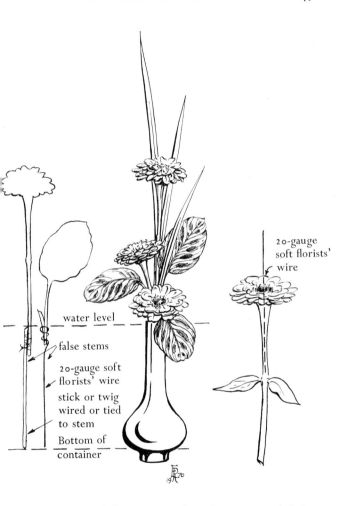

water level

false stems

20-gauge soft
florists' wire

stick or twig
wired or tied
to stem

Bottom of
container

20-gauge
soft florists'
wire

16 Arrangement of three zinnias, three dracaena (or gladioli)
leaves and three maranta leaves

My arrangement of three zinnias (drawing no. 16) is very simple. It consists of three zinnia flowers, three maranta (*M. leuconeura massangeana*) leaves taken from one of my houseplants (condition these first by total immersion) and three gladioli, dracaena or other spikey leaves. As I have already mentioned, you can raise a flower or leaf to the required height by tying, wiring or taping a false stem to it. Do, however, make sure that the actual end of the flower or leaf can drink.

The pottery or glass-decanter-like bottle vase I have used provides the necessary base weight for this dramatic yet not too formal use of zinnias.

Three Carnations

'I can't have real flowers in my house—it's the central heating you know!' How often have we heard that said? Probably said it ourselves! There is no doubt that central heating is hard on flowers. It is a very dry heat, and to start with it draws all the moisture out of the surface of the flowers and foliage quicker than it can be replaced through the stems by the water in the container. A local humidity can be provided by spraying, which will reduce transpiration—the transfer of moisture to the atmosphere—to a considerable extent. Some of us will remember the dish of water our grandmothers placed in the hearth in front of the gas fire. This provided a degree of humidity which greatly added to the general comfort.

I have found that if flowers are well conditioned before arranging they will last well in quite a small depth of water. A shallow bowl with the flowers anchored in a pinholder is a case in point (see drawing no. 17). The comparatively large surface area of water provides a local humidity by evaporation which combats this transpiration.

17 Arrangement of three carnations and dracaena leaves

My arrangement uses only three flowers—carnations. Other flowers that are suitable for such 'economy' arrangements while the central heating is on include chrysanthemums, iris and tulips. Dracaena leaves (which I have used), iris foliage, eucalyptus, preserved beech and ferns are but a few of the foliages suitable for use in such arrangements. Bulrushes, too, can be used to good effect.

The pinholder, which should be stuck to the bottom of the bowl with Oasis Fix, can be hidden in a variety of ways. Pebbles, shells or moss are effective—particularly so are the large coloured glass 'rocks' obtainable from some florists.

A word of warning. Don't put carnations into stone-cold water, especially in winter. This causes premature curling—a pronounced shrinking of the flowers. To obtain the longest possible life condition carnations for an hour or so in lukewarm water, having, of course, cut the ends of the stems diagonally with a sharp knife.

10 Four-flower Arrangements

Four is not so difficult a number of flowers to arrange as we thought at first. In fact, with the right container and a few ancillary items, such as branches or leaves, it is really very simple.

Let us first consider four flowers without any additions. I have chosen four longiflorum or harrisii lilies (see drawing no. 18) and a large green-glass globe bowl. This, I feel, provides sufficient base weight for these long-stemmed large flowers. The only 'aid' I require is the smallest size pin-holder secured in the bottom of the bowl with Oasis Fix. This is to support the longest lily stem.

I have stripped sufficient of the leaves from the stems to accentuate the rhythm of their natural curves. It will be noticed that there are six stems in the glass bowl. This is because the lower leaves on the right and left are on the parts of the stems remaining after reducing the length of the lower two lilies.

Some prefer to arrange the flowers in the hand and to tie or secure them loosely with a rubber band. Obviously, the smaller the opening in the bowl, the less control of the stem that is necessary.

Four iris with suitable foliage can be turned into quite a satisfactory stylised arrangement. Drawing no. 19 shows such an arrangement in a flat cactus pan, using *Philodendron scandens* leaves with 'Golden Harvest' iris. The latter are a robust flower and, apart from having a sweet scent, generally have a second bud which develops as the first flower

18   Arrangement of four longiflorum or harrisii lilies in a glass
     globe bowl

fades. Thus it is possible to have an arrangement that will
last for a week or more.

The pan was matt-glazed a bluish green and, with the
strong yellow of the iris and the yellow green of the
Philodendron scandens leaves, a very pleasant complementary
colour harmony resulted.

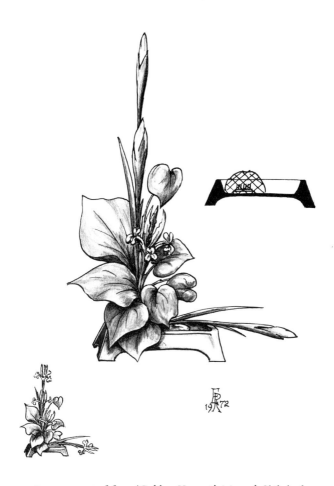

19 Arrangement of four 'Golden Harvest' iris and *Philodendron scandens* leaves in a flat cactus pan

11 Fives and Tens

For years we British have thought in terms of dozens and half-dozens. We always thought of a bunch of flowers as being either one or the other. Decimalisation has altered all this. Flowers are now sold in bunches of fives and tens; the half-dozen and dozen bunch has long since gone the way of £ s. d.

To those who have no gardens and are dependent on the florist for their flowers this loss of one or two in a bunch may seem to present some difficulties in arranging. This need not be the case, however, for with a little thought and planning I think we can get very nearly as good an effect with ten flowers as with twelve, and even with five instead of six.

Drawing no. 20, which shows an arrangement of six tulips, is a case in point. If the bottom right-hand tulip is removed, you will see that the remaining five make quite a reasonable arrangement. It now becomes symmetrical instead of being asymmetrical. Try the effect of removing this one tulip by placing a finger over it.

Compare the arrangement of twelve daffodils shown in drawing no. 21 on page 56 with that of ten daffodils shown in drawing no. 22 on page 57. You can see that the use of ten daffodils has not greatly upset the appearance or balance of the basic arrangement. It is now a little more triangulated, but the general rhythm has not been upset and placement is very similar.

The answer to the problem is planning, as indeed it is to the successful making of any arrangement. You must first

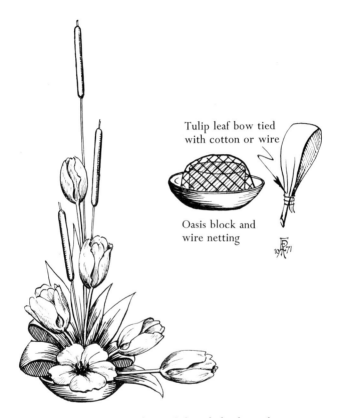

Tulip leaf bow tied
with cotton or wire

Oasis block and
wire netting

20   Arrangement of six tulips and three bulrushes. This arrange-
     ment can be achieved with five tulips by omitting the bottom
     right-hand flower

decide on the vase or bowl you think most suitable for both
the flowers and the surroundings, and then do the arrangement in your mind's eye.

21   Arrangement of twelve daffodils

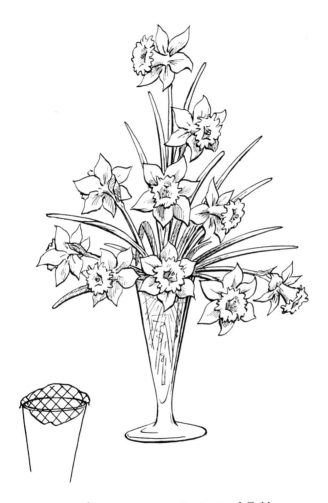

22   The same arrangement using ten daffodils

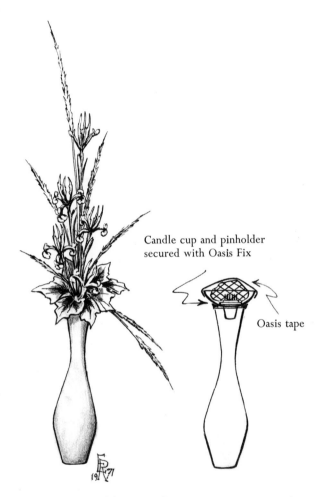

Candle cup and pinholder
secured with Oasis Fix

Oasis tape

23 Arrangement of five iris and water grass; marengo ivy leaves
conceal the mechanics

Five Iris

Nowadays the iris is almost an all-the-year-round flower. In fact, there is hardly one month in twelve when the blue iris—'Wedgewood' or 'Van Vleit'—cannot be bought. The white and yellow (some varieties of the latter are very sweet-scented) are, however, still restricted to the spring and summer.

Drawing no. 23 illustrates a simple but effective way of arranging one bunch of iris. The white, matt-glazed bottle vase is most attractive in line and shape but not, at first sight, at all easy for flower arrangement. A candle cup held in position by a ring of Oasis Fix round the top of the vase, a pinholder and a ball of crumpled wire netting have, however, solved the problem. Instead of the water grasses, trimmed beech or pussy willow could be used. Flag iris foliage or dracaena are other alternatives.'

The mechanics are concealed by a 'rosette' of large variegated marengo ivy leaves. This plant will grow well in any odd corner of the garden. In fact, most of the ivies sold as houseplants will grow out of doors. The miniatures are particularly useful to the flower arranger.

Five Cyclamen

My little arrangement of five cyclamen (see drawing no. 24) is interesting because, contrary to general belief, cyclamen last well as a cut flower. So, if you lose the leaves of one of your plants (probably from overwatering), don't throw it away; let the buds develop and, as they do, use them in an arrangement. Unfortunately, the stems do not reach their full length until the bud is fully open, and thus an arrangement of cyclamen must generally be composed of the larger, taller flowers

being above or higher than the smaller ones. This is quite
contrary to general practice, but as that is the way cyclamen
grow I see no reason to argue and have arranged them

24   Arrangement of five cyclamen flowers, buds and leaves

accordingly. The other interesting feature of this arrangement
is that the focal point is a void, framed in a cradle of cyclamen leaves. Another cyclamen flower could have been added
at this point, but I don't think this would have resulted
in any great improvement.

   It is not generally known that there are a number of hardy
varieties of cyclamen that will do well in all but the coldest

areas. They should be planted in rich leaf-mould in September for spring (February–April) flowering and in June or
July for autumn flowering.

25 Movement—just five cyclamen flowers

A Daffodil for Saint David?

Why and when did this lovely spring flower become a rival
to the leek as the national emblem of Wales? I have searched
without much success.

In searching I have learned that Saint David was the son of the Prince of Cardiganshire and an uncle of King Arthur; and that there is a particular daffodil (*Narcissus obvallaris*), known as the Tenby daffodil, growing wild in Pembrokeshire and other parts of the Principality. By the way, did you know that daffodils are not indigenous to North Wales?

I now know all about the leek (in Welsh *cennin cyffredin*) which, according to Shakespeare, adorned the helmet of Fluellen. Also, and this is strange, that in parts of Wales the daffodil is called *cennin Pedr* (Saint Peter's leek) and in others *blodau Dewi* or *cennin Dewi* (David's flower *or* David's leek). I also learned that the leek was sacred in ancient Egypt—and that in the Cornish and Breton languages it was *cenin* and *kinen*. But nowhere could I find out much about the daffodil.

It seems that, since the times of the early Romano Britons (they were not savages), the leek has been part of a ritual of recognition and friendship. Henry Tudor's men wore it at the Battle of Bosworth. Because the plucked leek is green and white, these colours were adopted as the background of the Welsh national flag with the red dragon of Wessex. So we have the leek for the soldiers and the rugby men of Wales, but what of the daffodil?

The first recorded incident of the ceremonial presentation of this flower was by King George V to Edward, Prince of Wales, during the investiture at Caernarvon in 1911. The green and white of the pulled daffodil stem is similar to the leek; apparently the bloom was ignored.

Anyway, whether spring is early or late, on or about Saint David's day somewhere in the Principality we are pretty sure to see in parks, on motorway verges, in woods or on the hillsides carpets of these lovely golden flowers, their little trumpets proclaiming that Wales is the land of song and poetry.

26 Ten daffodils arranged in a brandy balloon; coloured glass
marbles conceal the mechanics

Daffodils are not difficult to arrange, and if 'cut hard', just
out of the bud stage, they will develop and last very well in
water. Unlike many other flowers, particularly those with
'woody' stems, daffodils require little conditioning before
arranging; cutting the ends of the stems is all that is

necessary. Do make sure, however, when buying daffodils in bud that they really are quite fresh. If they are stale, buds will not open.

Drawing no. 26 shows an arrangement of the now average bunch of daffodils: ten stems, three of which are in bud, plus a few foliage spikes. The 'container' is a small brandy balloon. The mechanics—a small pinholder secured with Oasis Fix—are hidden by a couple of dozen coloured marbles.

Part 2—Winter and Spring

12 Winter Fragrance

To me Twelfth Night, 6 January, is always the beginning of the New Year. It is the day when traditionally all the Christmas decorations are taken down; the holly and the mistletoe are burned, giving a delicious woodland smoky smell (a little ceremony soon to be a thing of the past as the open fire disappears); and the Christmas tree is stripped of its colour and sparkle, and is relegated—if we are lucky enough to have a rooted one—to some shady corner of the garden to be dug up again next Christmas.

So, the house is back to normal. Now, what of the garden? Is there anything in it for the flower arranger? Something must be found to take the place of that 'Christmassy' arrangement we were so proud of—a good deal of which can be saved for next year if carefully wrapped and stored in a dry place.

At first sight there seems little, if anything, in the garden, and obviously flowers from the florist will not be cheap, so we must think of some compromise that will ensure the maximum effect from the minimum of flowers.

Actually, no single month in the garden need be entirely lacking in colour as far as trees and shrubs are concerned, and December and January are no exception. Winter jasmine (*Jasminum nudiflorum*), winter sweet (*Chimonanthus fragrans*) and witch hazel (*Hamamelis mollis*) flower from December to February. These are fragrant, particularly witch hazel with its primrose scent which becomes more intense indoors. *Viburnum fragrans* is another shrub that

Dome of 2-in wire mesh   Pinholder secured with
                          Oasis Fix

27   Winter arrangement of winter jasmine, winter sweet, witch
hazel, hart's tongue fern and Christmas roses

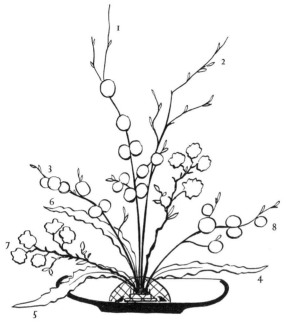

28 How to do it. Diagram showing the order of placement of the branches and hart's tongue fern for this winter arrangement; the Christmas roses are placed afterwards

provides both colour and fragrance from the winter garden. If protected with cloches, long-stemmed, unsullied Christmas roses (*Helleborus niger*) will be available for cutting, and you might possibly find a snowdrop or two poking through.

The arrangement illustrated in drawings nos. 27 and 28 is very easy to do. The mechanics are simply a large pinholder (3-inch diameter), secured with Oasis Fix, and a dome of crumpled wire netting. After you have arranged your branches, ferns and flowers according to the numbers, cover the mechanics with stones, moss or a suitable short foliage.

13 Church Flowers begin with Easter

Easter is the most important festival of the Christian year, and surely the loveliest. The birds are busy. Almond and cherry blossom abound. There are Easter eggs and bunnies, and Easter bonnets, and the young man's fancy. . . . ! The name 'Easter' is derived from Eostre, the Anglo-Saxon goddess of Spring, and much of this lovely festival dates back to pagan times. The egg was the symbol of life and fertility. The breaking of the chick through the shell was later taken as a symbol of Christ's resurrection.

Did you know that Easter Day is fixed by an Act of Parliament? In 1752 it was decreed that it should be the first Sunday after the full moon around the twenty-first day of March—a hypothetical full moon too! Easter is also inextricably mixed up with the Jewish Passover.

Easter is the time when flowers again appear in church after the long austerity of Lent and seem to provide a confirmation that winter is really past. Now the flower arranger can really be quite profligate in the use of flowers and foliage.

One of the most satisfying things for the flower arranger to do is the flowers in church. Yet why is it so often left to the few dedicated members of the altar guilds or other such committees? Surely it can only be nervousness, which is really quite unwarranted because the same basic rules apply, with perhaps an extra emphasis on scale. Lighting and background may also require a greater degree of consideration, but I can assure you that there is no need for undue apprehension.

29 Flower decorations for a wedding in the twelfth-century church of St. Edeyrns in the parish of Llanedeyrn, Wales

Whatever the denomination, I find a peace and tranquillity in the House of God which it is difficult to find anywhere else. This influence is, to me, particularly strong in an empty church, and I think that whether you are a gifted and experienced amateur or a professional, an apprentice or a ham-fisted beginner, and whether the flowers are for a wedding, a christening, the Harvest Festival or any other special occasion, you too will be influenced. I also think that on such occasions you will do better flower arrangements than you had ever thought yourself capable of. Of one thing I am certain, and that is that you will have gained an hour or so of complete relaxation.

I have decorated a number of churches—some, many, many times—but I always sit for a while in the middle and absorb the atmosphere before I begin arranging, and although you may have known your church from childhood I advise you to do the same. This will ensure that you are fully aware of dominant features and any little changes that may have passed unnoticed. The dominant features are generally functional and often of great beauty, and your decoration should enhance them, never distract from them.

When I am satisfied that I have fully considered every aspect with the lights on and off, I like to go out and come in again as if I were a member of the congregation. I pause at the door and note which particular features, if any, have an immediate impact upon me. These should, of course, be the chancel and the altar, and all decoration should lead the eye to this focal point.

There are, of course, exceptions. Llandaff Cathedral, Cardiff, is one. Here Epstein's Majestas—Christ in ascendance—is the dominant feature. The somewhat controversial concrete supporting arches, however, provide a frame for the high altar seen beyond, and it seems right and proper

30 Church flowers

that all major ceremonies should take place under this impressive and, to me, beautiful symbol. Any floral decoration here must, in my opinion, be particularly restrained.

On the other hand, your church may be one of those dear little intimate places whose origin goes back into local antiquity, where squints and leper's windows and beautiful wrought iron or brass standards, which once supported candles or oil lamps, still remain. Here little restraint seems necessary, and country or garden flowers with trailing ivies, ferns and creepers are particularly appropriate. Even in such places, however, do not cover up beautiful things just for the sake of it. 'Paint not the lily nor gild refined gold' is a saying that is particularly applicable in such cases. Your flower arrangements should draw attention to beautiful things and away from the unsightly.

14 Lilies

The severe beauty of the arum lily, with the perfect curves of its spathe or trumpet, is surely at its best and most effective in line or stylised arrangements. The stems, which are reasonably pliable, can be straightened or curved as you wish by gentle manipulation using the warmth of the hand.

The leaves are particularly beautiful. They are best conditioned by complete immersion for a few hours before arranging. There is a tendency for the tips to flag quickly unless they are properly conditioned.

Arum buds are effective too, but I know of no way of opening them (unlike *L. rubrum*, *L. longiflorum*, etc.) other than to a limited degree with the finger. Hot water treatment will revive arums but has no effect on the development of the blooms, which remain completely inert after cutting. The stems, like those of daffodils, have a distinct tendency to split and curl outwards at the ends. This makes arrangement difficult, particularly if they are to be supported by a pinholder, and because of their extreme sappiness they are easily frayed by wire netting. If, however, a couple of inches at the end are bound with tape (and left open to permit the intake of water) and fixed with cotton or a coil or two of thin wire, the stems will be sufficiently durable to be poked into Oasis or Florapak and there will be no difficulty with a pinholder. Arum leaves do not have quite such a tendency to split, but they should be cut at a distinctly sharp angle.

Arums have always been popular flowers for church decoration, especially in Wales and particularly at Easter.

Recently, however, harrisii and longiflorum lilies have become much more popular. In the opinion of many, they are much more decorative (after all they are called the Easter lily) and, since every bud will open in water (arums will not), they really are much better value.

31   Arum lilies on the altar

In my opinion, it depends on circumstances and situations how and which of these two lovely flowers you use. A stylised pair of matching arrangements of arums each side of an altar cross can have a particularly dramatic effect in a modern setting. However, in a more traditional setting, triangular or circular arrangements of harrisii or longiflorum lilies in the conventional brass altar vases seem to me much more suitable. These flowers are also far more effective in large, massed pedestal arrangements. They are easy to arrange and require little, if any, extra foliage. They can also be mixed with so many other flowers—iris, tulips, chrysanthemums and carnations to name but a few. Arums, on the other hand, are generally best used by themselves and, because of the clear-cut lines of both their foliage and their flowers, considerable care and some skill in arranging is necessary if the best effect is sought.

Drawing no. 31 shows a suggested matching pair of arum arrangements, placed one each side of a silver altar cross. Such arrangements are comparatively economical, seven flowers only being required for each arrangement. The flower stems should be 'hand humoured' to the required curves. I usually insert a 12-inch long, 18-gauge wire up the centre of the stems to ensure that the desired curves will not be affected by any changes in temperature or by the influence of light from any one particular direction. The dracaena, yucca or New Zealand flax leaves are also 'hand humoured' to the curves you want. These, I find, keep to the curves induced. The three loops are tied with wire, or with cotton if you haven't any wire. Note how I have turned the top two arums so that the spathes have their undersides to the front. This, I think, heightens the illusion of ascending.

The Madonna lily (*Lilium candidum*), whose cultivation

32   Arrangement of lilies (*L. candidum*, *L. regale* and *L. longiflorum*),
     bamboo and a cut fan palm

goes back nearly four centuries and which is so much associated with Christian symbolism, is a genus of over eighty species with countless varieties. *L. candidum* was the only English garden lily until the mid-sixteenth century. The genus is confined to the Northern Hemisphere, where it is distributed in a ring within the temperate zone.

The growing of most lilies is not difficult; all prefer a soil that is well drained and fairly rich, containing plenty of humus. As most grow well with rhododendrons and azaleas, it would seem they prefer a slightly acid soil. A few varieties, however, do not dislike lime, though all require good drainage. Some like their heads in full sun, but all need a cool root run, and so the root area should be shaded from strong sun by low-growing plants.

The arrangement on page 78, drawing no. 32, shows three very popular lilies. *L. candidum* and *L. regale* are quite hardy. The third, *L. longiflorum*—the Easter lily—is best grown under glass. The cut fan palm not only provides an anchorage for the somewhat stiff stems of the lilies but also seems to continue the rhythm of the swirling motif in the vase.

15 Lily of the Valley

Lily of the valley (*Convallaria majalis*) is surely one of the sweetest of flowers. In form and scent it is unrivalled, except perhaps by the rose, but then the two are so different that I think there can be no true comparison except for the intensity of their delicious perfumes.

In March and April the leaves begin to appear (flowering late April and May), and have you noticed how lily of the valley seems to prefer to live the hard way? Often, irrespective of the direction of sun and shade, and, it seems, ignoring good, rich, prepared soil, you will find it forcing its way through asphalt, gravel and even concrete paths. I suppose it must be something to do with its very long roots. Anyway, I have found it prefers to be left undisturbed and go its own way until the quality of the flowers deteriorates. Thus it finds very little favour with the formal gardener.

I have said elsewhere that for me one of life's small luxuries is to enter a room perfumed with the scent of roses massed in large bowls. I think that bowls of lily of the valley must be added to this. Large bowls of snowdrops and prim-roses, though they have no scent, affect me in much the same way. Perhaps this is because they are intimate but inde-pendent little flowers which are always at their best when growing wild.

Years ago in parts of Monmouthshire in the Wye Valley, even beside a main road, I have seen wooded slopes carpeted white with lily of the valley. The bluebells that also grew there in plenty are still to be seen, but the lily of the valley

Oasis round
and 'frog'

33   A bowl of lily of the valley; variegated ivy trails conceal the
     mechanics in front

now have to be searched for. I suppose this is another of the
tolls exacted by the ubiquitous motor car.

For those who do not have to count the cost, lily of the
valley is available all the year round at the florist. The leaves
and stems are a much lighter green than those of lily of the
valley grown out of doors and the perfume is not quite so
intense. Both last comparatively well as cut flowers, although
I find outdoor lily of the valley requires considerable conditioning if not put into water immediately it is cut. Sometimes it is even necessary to use the hot water treatment.

16 An Easter Basket

The abundance of fresh spring flowers in bloom at Easter is one of the most pleasant signs that winter is finally over. There are plenty available both in the garden and from the florist.

Easter eggs are very much a part of this lovely festival and Easter Sunday morning breakfast is quite an occasion. In my family—and I expect in countless thousands of others—it was, and still is, a family affair. Coming back from early service the sun always seemed to shine brighter, the birds to be busier and more full of song, and the coffee and toast to smell much more appetising than usual. We always had little presents at Easter (still do!) and, of course, brightly coloured boiled eggs. I expect you know that only vegetable (culinary) dyes should be used. My mother always did something special as a table-centre, and always with something from the garden. We had no florist near us and, in any case, I doubt whether the family budget would have stretched to buying flowers.

An attractive and quite easy to do Easter basket table-centre is illustrated in drawing no. 34. The 'basket' is made from an oval plastic fruit tray. These trays can be purchased in black or white, and it is a very simple matter to paint one any colour you like. The handle is made from a 3-foot length of stout wire, or a hazel twig covered with coloured cellophane, crepe paper or ribbon and then carefully bent to the required curve. The two ends are tied together with string or wire about 4 inches apart and then wired to the tray

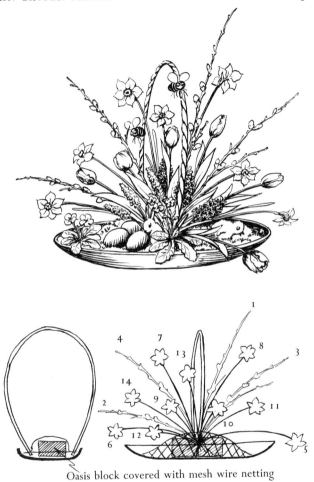

Oasis block covered with mesh wire netting

34 An Easter basket, comprising pussy willow, 'Actaea' narcissi, tulips, hyacinths, muscari, a primrose plant and two polyanthus plants

(make holes in the plastic tray with a red-hot knitting needle). The Oasis block is then secured in position by pressing it down onto the tying wire.

My arrangement is composed of pussy willow (catkins could be used instead), ten narcissi ('Actaea') and six tulips. From the garden I dug up a primrose and two polyanthus, and cut six stems of muscari (grape hyacinth) and three stems of hyacinths. Many florists sell the little bees or butterflies, but they are not difficult to make yourself.

My drawing obviously shows only one side of this table-centre. Narcissi nos. 9, 10 and 11 (see numbered diagram) will be on the other side, as will the other three stems of muscari, three more eggs and another Easter bunny. The tulips and hyacinths are arranged diagonally across the centre of the tray. The wire netting and the Oasis block—the mechanics—are covered with bun moss or clean shingle. Finally, the eggs, chick and bunnies are placed in position.

Follow the numbers to obtain the basic shape and then add the remainder as convenient. I use a pointed stick or a wooden meat skewer to make the necessary holes in the Oasis for the soft-stemmed narcissi and muscari.

Part 3—Summer Flowers from the Garden and the Florist

17 'Til May Be Out!

The old country saying that begins 'cast ne'er a clout . . .' is frequently misquoted as ''til May be out'. But actually the saying is 'cast ne'er a clout 'til *the* may be out'—a subtle difference which, if you think about it, makes good sense.

The may or hawthorn (*Crataegus oxyacantha*) is among the last of our spring-flowering trees and shrubs to come into full bloom. North, south, east and west in this country, it is generally unwise to plant out geraniums—and, in fact, the great majority of the popular bedding plants—until both the ground and the air are warm enough. The may or hawthorn will not bloom until it is. The various prunus (Japanese cherry), the magnolia and the apple blossom are not so cautious, and are often in full splendour in early April and May only to be ravaged by cold winds, sleet and driving rain, and even to be touched by a late frost.

It is not generally appreciated that these beautiful trees and shrubs make delightful house decorations. But they must be cut in full bud and properly conditioned before they are arranged. They will then develop in water and will last for some days. Of course, there is a tendency to drop a few petals, but to my mind this is a small price to pay. And as the blossoms fade, so delicate young leaves will unfurl and develop. This opening of buds and the appearance of the young green is, to me, a most exciting thing. Have you noticed how, as the days get longer and the sun begins to have more warmth, there is a warm glow—a pinky flush—that seems to radiate from the trees and bushes? This is the

35   Arrangement of magnolia and 'Kanzan' prunus

loosening of the bud cases which have protected the young shoots throughout the rigours of winter. At this time of the year almost anything cut and brought indoors will develop 'sticky buds'—horse chestnut, larch, beech, forsythia.

Magnolia blooms, like gardenia, bruise easily, but this can be overcome if they are cut in full bud and then conditioned for an hour or so by complete immersion in luke-warm water. The buds can then be gently opened—but be sure to do so when they are wet, and with wet fingers, and then they should not bruise.

Magnolias are woodland plants, and therefore prefer cool and sheltered positions. Most of the prunus, however, do better in an open, sunny situation in well-drained soil, and they will do well in lime. Plant prunus from October to February. If your garden soil is poor, you should well pre-pare the site beforehand. Dig a hole at least 18 inches deep and the same diameter, and fill it with two parts John Innes No. 2 and one part peat. A good leaf-mould will do equally well. As time goes on, mulch magnolias well to preserve the acidity they prefer. There are some varieties of magnolia that will grow on chalk, but be sure to check up on this before planting.

Your local nurseryman or garden centre nowadays has a large variety of container-grown flowering shrubs and trees, most of which can be planted at any time. They will gladly advise you on cultivation.

By the way, gardenias and camellias are much more hardy than is generally believed, and now take their place with the rhododendron and azalea. Apart from their lovely flowers, they are unrivalled as a source of beautiful evergreen foliage.

In the arrangement illustrated in drawing no. 35 I have used four branches of prunus (double-flowered, deep pink 'Kanzan') and two magnolia buds, with one fully-opened magnolia flower as the focal point. The mechanics comprise a large pinholder secured with Oasis Fix.

18 The Beauty of the Rose

Throughout recorded history the rose has exerted a significant religious and aesthetic influence. The Medes and the Persians, the Egyptians, the Greeks and the Romans used it for decoration at feasts and banquets. The Crusaders brought sweet-scented roses from Damascus. Attar (essence) of roses, which is derived from the essential oil of roses, probably originated from ancient Persia. Red and white roses were used respectively by the Lancastrians and Yorkists as badges in the Civil War. Down the ages the poets have sung the praises of the form and fragrance of the rose. It seems always to have been regarded as the 'Queen of Flowers' and the red rose as the symbol of love.

One of the most versatile of shrubs, the rose produces tremendously decorative fruits, the hips, which provide a source of vitamin C (rose-hip syrup was of great value to innumerable babies of our nation in World War II). How beautiful, too, is rose foliage, with its varied shape and texture. Did you know that rose water is distilled from the leaves of roses?

It is possible, with careful selection, to have roses blooming continuously from about May to early winter. And did you realise that the countless varieties available today are derived from the sweet briar (*Rosa rubiginosa*) and the dog rose (*Rosa canina*)? It is impossible to say when hybridising first began, but the story of the production and present perfection of the hybrid tea, floribunda, bud-climber and rambler is more full of romance, frustration and failure,

36   Arrangement of five long-stemmed roses

tears and success than that of any other cultivated flower. Names that spring to mind are Dixon, Meilland, McGredy and Wheatcroft.

Roses last well as a cut flower. To obtain the longest possible life they should be cut when just about to open and then properly conditioned before arranging.

I like to remove all surplus foliage, and all thorns should be removed as well. Not only does this make handling much more comfortable but it also ensures that other blooms and foliage are not torn when more roses are inserted in the arrangement.

To return to conditioning. Split the bottom of the stems up for about 2 inches. Some people prefer to crush them, but I think this is a little messy. Flagging roses can be revived by placing the ends of the stems in about 2 inches of very hot water for two or three minutes and then plunging them into deep cold water. However, I prefer to lay them flat in cold water—blooms and all—for as long as necessary. Roses with 'hanging heads' and 'dried up' foliage will revive and last for two or three days after a few hours of such treatment.

Drawing no. 36 shows a vase of long-stemmed roses. ('Cutting long' during the first flush is, as I have said before, good for your bushes.) For such beautiful flowers as these no 'aid' is necessary in this narrow-necked vase.

19 Columbine

Columbine, or aquilegia to give it its botanical name, is a perennial that I consider warrants a place in any garden. It crosses so easily that there are now an incalculable number of hybrids. The colours and colour combinations seem almost infinite, ranging from clear yellow, mauve and violet through a multitude of pastel pinks and crimson to scarlet. The perianth petals and spurs resemble an eagle's claw, hence the probable origin of the name from *aquila*, the Latin for 'eagle'.

The foliage, too, is attractive and, like the flower, despite a very thin stem remains erect and lasts well in water if cut hard, i.e. when just in full bloom.

Most varieties are hardy, though some require a little protection in winter. *Aquilegia skinneri*—the Mexican columbine—bicoloured yellow and scarlet, is a little more delicate than some. All soils suit aquilegia, but they do prefer some degree of richness. Generally, they do better in partial shade. If planted in full sun, give them the protection of other, slightly taller, plants; this will prevent root baking.

The little arrangement I have illustrated in drawing no. 37 is in a French mustard pot that we couldn't bear to throw away. It is cream glazed pottery and is decorated in three sections: the name etc., a basket-work panel and a third panel (not shown) of a flower design. The colour of the figuring and decoration is sepia and a warm brown.

The points that should be noted about this arrangement are its economy (only five stems of flowers were cut) and

that the focal point has been achieved by careful positioning
of the euonymus foliage. This member of the laurel family is
a most useful bush to have in the garden. Its variegated cream
and delicate green foliage is very attractive and is available
for cutting all the year round.

Crumpled
wire netting

37 Columbine and euonymus foliage, which provides the
focal point, arranged in a French mustard pot

20 Clematis

Clematis, surprisingly, lasts well as a cut flower, despite its thin, wire-like stem. With its many species and variety of colour and size (it has from four to eight petals), it is one of the prettiest climbers we can see in the garden.

Blooming from April to September, it will grow well in almost any soil, situation and even aspect, climbing among other things such as wisteria, pyracantha and roses. Most clematis can be grown in the open, too—up poles or old tree stumps. They do not like draughts or the soil to become hot sun-baked at their roots. A mulching of half-decayed leaves or dung will prevent the soil from drying out and will keep the roots cool.

Clematis in considerable variety can be purchased at reasonable prices in pots or attractive cellophane packs from most florists and garden centres.

Drawing no. 38 shows how to make a simple arrangement of clematis in a shallow bowl or soup plate, using a medium-sized (2-inch) pinholder for stem support. Oasis can, of course, be used, but the concealing of it tends to make the base of the arrangement somewhat clumsy. The thin stems need not present any difficulty in fixing into the spikes of the pinholder if a packing piece of another, thicker, stem is used like a kind of wedge. Alternatively, a leaf can be wrapped round the end of a thin stem to make it the required thickness. Or a short piece of a thicker stem can be tied to the main stem. A few stones—coloured if you like—or moss can

Wedges

Stems wedged in
pins with another
larger, stem

38   Arrangement of clematis in a shallow bowl

be arranged around the pinholder to hide the mechanics. It really is very simple.

Clematis make a lovely decoration for the centre of a dinner table, using trails of its own foliage to link the main arrangement to smaller ones each side.

By the way, did you know there is a comparatively new variety which has little bell-shaped flowers?

21 Antirrhinum

The antirrhinum, or snapdragon, gets its name from the Greek *anti* meaning 'like' and *rhinos* meaning 'snout'—and that is a fair description when you think of the upper and lower lips opening when squeezed at the sides to form a mouth and a pouch behind. In company with the buttercup and the daisy, I suppose this flower must live in the childhood memories of almost everybody. I am still fascinated by the sight of a large bumble-bee opening what we as children called 'the bunnies' mouths'.

This plant originally came from the Mediterranean region, where it grows to 3 feet in height. A half-hardy annual, many garden varieties have been developed by natural variation, and it has been hybridised to produce plants in a wide range of colour and of various heights. There are even antirrhinums for rock gardens—*A. asarina* and *A. glutinosum*. These are of a trailing habit and have yellow and creamy flowers. In some districts antirrhinums will prove hardy and will remain perennial, but generally they become straggly after the first year, so it is best to treat them as annuals.

I find antirrhinums quite a good cut flower if well conditioned. A good long drink in a cool place is essential and, as with larkspur, lupin, foxglove and suchlike, a couple of tablespoonsful of granulated sugar in the water will to a considerable extent stop the dropping of the florets.

A new double variety has just appeared. The traditional lips or snout have almost vanished and in their place at the end of the trumpet or throat a 2-inch diameter double row

39 Three stems of the new double variety of antirrhinum
    arranged in a jug with a boss of hydrangea, four hydrangea buds
    and a few leaves. The familiar single variety of antirrhinum is
    shown inset

of frills has appeared. This new variety is particularly useful as a cut flower; it grows to a height of just over 2 feet and has a wide range of colours, including a lovely peachy pink.

Drawing no. 39 shows an arrangement of three stems of this new antirrhinum (one can hardly call it a snapdragon) arranged in a jug with a large boss of hydrangea bloom, four hydrangea buds and a few large leaves. Crumpled wire netting is the best form of stem support for this arrangement.

Note the comparison between this new variety and the original (inset) antirrhinum. Why not try it?

22 Border Carnations and Veronica

These two garden flowers are long lasting and quite easy to arrange. The carnations have stems up to 18 inches long and each stem usually has a number of buds, many of which will open in water. The pink and mauve veronicas (*V. spicata* and *V. incana*) have long elegant spikes of bloom growing 18 inches to 2 feet high. There are about 250 species of veronica; most of these are easy to grow and their flowering period spreads from June to August. They have been known for centuries and can be found in the Caucasus, Greece, France and Britain, and even as far afield as Japan.

Almost any type of container is suitable (providing the proportions are correct) for these flowers, and once they have started 'drinking' they will stand in quite shallow water.

The container I have used in the arrangement shown in drawing no. 40 is a lager glass. The proportions are elegant and, provided that the arrangement is technically correct, I like to see the stems of the flowers through the refracted light of the clear glass. To achieve this two things are essential. First, the mechanics must not show and, secondly, all stems must appear to converge on and emerge from a common area of origin—the focal area.

The aid or mechanics in this case is merely a little dome of wire netting, 1-inch mesh. A square of about 8 inches is simply doubled and folded to make a dome the same diameter as the top of the glass. This is placed so that it sits about half an inch down into the glass with two or three

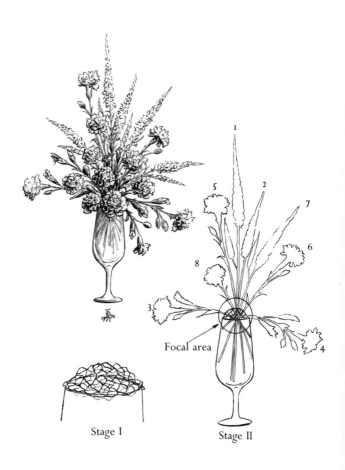

1

5   2

7

8   6

3

Focal area

4

Stage I   Stage II

40   Border carnations and veronica arranged in a lager glass

short ends outside—like clips. Now, with a pencil or small pointed stick—a large knitting needle is a useful 'tool'— poke through the wire netting at various angles; this will help you in your eventual placement of the flowers. This 'tool' will be most useful to you throughout the whole period of arranging.

Having made sure that your flowers are properly conditioned and that all unwanted foliage has been carefully stripped from the stems, proceed with the arrangement. It is quite simple—just follow the numbers. Be careful, though, that you do not cut too much off the stems of nos. 1, 2, 5, 6 and 7. These not only provide the image or design seen through the glass but they also give vertical stability.

The addition of 'Chrysal', a powder additive obtainable from florists, will ensure longer lasting, as well as preventing the premature dropping of the minute veronica florets (as, to a lesser degree, does the addition of sugar).

Brandy balloons in various colours of glass are popular flower containers. You can obtain the effect of coloured glass with clear-glass balloons by adding a suitable culinary vegetable dye to the water. If you do not like to see the refracted images of the stems through the glass, you can line the brandy balloon with crumpled kitchen foil. This gives a crackled or crystalline effect—silver or coloured as you wish, according to whether or not you colour the water.

23 Pinks

The dainty, sweet-scented pink (*Dianthus plumarius*)—like the border carnation (*Dianthus caryophyllus*), which is sometimes known as the florist's pink—is a must in the garden of anyone who likes to cut and arrange their own flowers.

The name 'dianthus' derives from the Greek *dios* meaning 'god' or 'divine' and *anthos* meaning 'flower'—'divine flower', 'flower of Zeus (*or* Jupiter)'. I learn that *D. caryophyllus* was described by a Greek writer in 300 B.C., and John Gerard wrote in 1597 of 'a wild creeping pink which groweth in our pastures near about London'. The name 'pink' has nothing to do with colour, it is an old English word meaning 'eye'. The large majority of pinks have a very distinct eye in the centre. 'Mrs. Sinkins' is perhaps the most famous of our garden pinks, and this is sweet-smelling, double and completely white; the 'eye' has been lost with development.

Dianthus plumarius is probably the parent of all our hybrid pinks. A native of South Eastern Europe and North Africa, it was introduced into the British Isles in 1629. It grows wild on sunny cliffs and well-drained hillsides, and thus it is too much to expect it to survive in cold, damp places where the soil is heavy. A rich, slightly friable loam is best. Dianthus are lime lovers.

While generally regarded as perennials, pinks are best treated as biennials in order to maintain the highest possible quality of perfection. Sow seed or take cuttings in April or early May, planting out in October or March. With most

41 Mixed pinks arranged in a glass trumpet vase with two pieces of rose foliage

varieties no artificial heat is required, a cold frame providing sufficient protection. Personally, I prefer to buy named plants from a reliable source.

These intimate little flowers are easy to arrange, particularly in one of those elegant, small, glass trumpet vases. They are attractive by themselves or with other flowers, and with or without any other foliage. The other day my wife made a most pleasing arrangement with a small bunch of show pinks 'Timothy' I had bought her and spikes of sorrel she had picked in our nearby fields. She put these in a tall lager glass, and the rusty rose tones of the sorrel greatly enhanced the delicate salmon-pink of the flowers.

Drawing no. 41 shows a simple arrangement of mixed pinks in a very elegant little glass trumpet vase. The proportions of this vase are so good that no aid is required to hold the flowers in position. To obtain an artistic effect all that is necessary is to blend your colours and vary the length of the stems.

24 Crown Imperial

This is the name given to the 'proud ones that weep for ever more'. According to legend, at Calvary only one flower would not bow its head as Jesus passed—the crown imperial. Ever afterwards it bowed its head in repentance with unshed tears in the form of its nectaries.

Fritillaria imperialis, to give the flower its proper botanical name, is an elegant plant. Its thick stem is crowned with a whorl of leaves, under which hangs a circle of bell-shaped blossoms, ranging in colour from a deep lemon- or butter-yellow to brick-red or reddish orange.

It is an excellent flower for arranging either singly or in groups. Growing up to 4 feet tall, it stands well in water, requiring no special conditioning other than the usual long drink. It should be noted, however, that this flower is not ideal for arrangements in small rooms, not only because of its size but also because it has a very strong scent, which some people might object to.

Crown imperial originates from Persia and Turkey. The plants are comparatively hardy, and will flourish and 'naturalise' in turf, preferring moist ground with heavy clay or the better loams. They should be periodically lifted and separated immediately they have died down after flowering, which is in late April and May. Crown imperial will also do well in sunny borders if surrounded by other plants, which will protect the bulbs from too much sun after the flowers have died down. They should be planted in the autumn

Oasis bowl with pinholder
secured to log with Oasis Fix

42   A single stem of crown imperial supported by a pinholder in
     an Oasis bowl placed on a log; the mechanics are hidden by
     large stones

at a depth of about 6 inches. They can, of course, also be grown in pots.

All things considered, the large bulbs (up to 4 inches in diameter) are not unduly expensive. Four good varieties are: *lutea maxima*, deep lemon-yellow; *chritralensis*, butter-yellow; 'Orange Brilliant', orange-lemon; and *rubra maxima*, burnt-orange-shaded red.

Drawing no. 42 shows a stem cut to about 24 inches. A large pinholder provides sufficient support. The bowl is hidden with stones or moss.

25 Acedanthera—the Abyssinian Lily

Acedanthera, or the Abyssinian lily as it is often called, belongs to the iris family. It produces small spikes of sweet-scented white flowers which have deep purple markings on five of their six petals.

It is available as a cut flower in August and is long lasting, six or more little flowers developing one after another on one stem and retaining their scent until the end. It grows in delightful curves and is well furnished with a number of deep green leaf spikes—a joy to the flower arranger.

For the arrangement shown in drawing no. 43 I have used three stems of acedanthera, which, if allowed to follow their own natural curves, will soon develop a rhythm all their own. Three leaf spikes and one *Bergenia cordifolia* leaf constitute the foliage material, and a 2-inch pinholder, some suitable stones or bun moss and a little figurine complete my requirements. Note the rhythm and balance of this very simple arrangement. The large bergenia leaf points to the focal point, which is provided by the little china heron, giving stability and balance.

Acedanthera are normally considered to be plants for cool greenhouses. In sheltered, mild districts one or two varieties, such as *A. bicolour murielae*, will do well if planted at the foot of a south-facing wall or fence. Acedanthera should be potted in leaf mould and sandy loam in equal proportions; keep them dry in dormant periods but well watered when growing. Plant out if desired in June, but bring them inside in early September for repotting. Propagation may be done by removing the little bulbs which will form round the main bulb or corm.

I hope this lovely flower will not go the way of so many and lose its perfume to meet the demands of mass production. It is certainly growing in popularity.

2-in pinholder secured
with Oasis Fix

43 Three stems of acedanthera (Abyssinian lily) arranged in a shallow bowl; a *Bergenia cordifolia* leaf provides balance and a little china heron the focal point

26 Anytime Gift—a Dozen or Ten Carnations

A dozen carnations and fern! Almost a standard gift to sweethearts, wives, mothers and others—and almost equally standard is the arranging, usually in a trumpet or other tall vase. All very easy, but not particularly imaginative.

Carnations are a useful flower used by themselves or with other flowers. They are available all the year round, and if we remember that they are really a summer flower they do last pretty well. Draughts and central heating are the most usual causes of premature wilting or shrivelling. Very few flowers will resist the latter unless they are frequently sprayed with water mist to produce a 'local humidity'. Never place carnations in cold water, particularly in winter.

I seldom use fern with carnations as I consider it interferes with the clarity of their line. Privet, forsythia or some other garden foliage is more in keeping.

Drawing no. 44 shows how to arrange a dozen carnations in a gold-fish bowl. Almost any other shape of 'container' can be used, provided that the proportions are correct, and Oasis, Florapak or wire netting can be used to hold the stems in the required position. I have used a small pin-holder, secured in the base of the bowl with Oasis Fix, and placed a circle of $1\frac{1}{2}$-inch mesh wire netting on the top of the bowl; this is secured with Sellotape. A lattice of Sellotape can be used if wire netting is not available. Make sure that the bowl is warm and dry before using Oasis Fix or Sellotape. Now just follow the numbers!

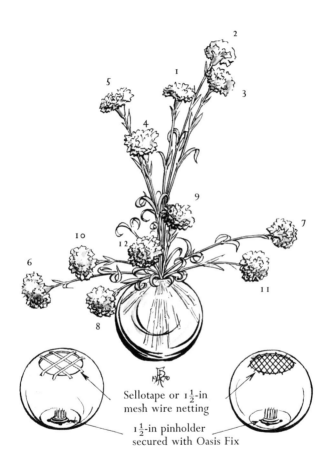

Sellotape or $1\frac{1}{2}$-in
mesh wire netting

$1\frac{1}{2}$-in pinholder
secured with Oasis Fix

44   Twelve carnations arranged in a gold-fish bowl—a good
     example of *balanced line*. This arrangement is also possible with
     ten carnations (omit flowers nos. 3 and 5)

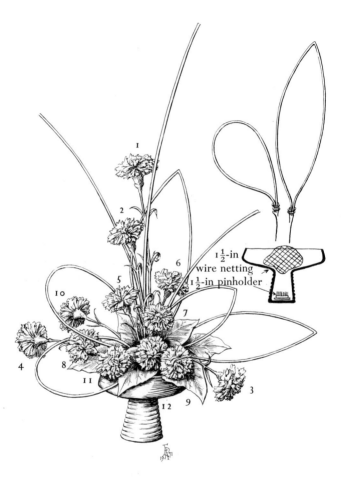

1½-in
wire netting
1½-in pinholder

45 Another way of arranging a dozen or ten carnations (omit
flowers nos. 6 and 10 if using ten carnations)

Carnation no. 1 is placed centrally and vertically. No. 2 leans slightly back and no. 4 slightly forwards, as do nos. 7 and 6 respectively. No. 8 projects well forwards. Be sure that nos. 1, 3 and 4 are long enough to reach the pinholder, thus ensuring stability. As always, be careful with the surplus stems or foliage. You will see that I have used one or two at the base and just behind the focal carnation (no. 12).

This is a good exercise in balanced line. Try it with other subjects. Balls of tissue paper tied onto privet or some other similar twigs are suitable and economical practice materials.

And, should you wish to keep pace with up-to-date ideas and think in metric terms, leave out nos. 3 and 5 and you have a ten-carnation arrangement.

Another way of arranging twelve carnations is shown in drawing no. 45. Here I have used a brownish green glazed pedestal bowl with a small pinholder and some crumpled wire netting. The basketry cane outline leaves are easy to make and their shape can be varied as you wish. Again, you can do this arrangement with ten carnations; nos. 6 and 10 are the flowers that should be omitted.

27 Freesia

Freesia, of South African origin, is surely one of the most useful of the small flowers available to the flower arranger. It is fragrant, long lasting and comes in a multitude of colours. As one flower fades another opens, and if the dead ones are carefully picked off a completely fresh appearance is preserved for four or five more days. The better-quality freesias (there are double and single varieties) have so many little flowers to a stem that those removed are hardly missed, and thus there is very little interference with the original arrangement.

Freesia is available from October to June; it requires no special conditioning and, except in the winter months, is comparatively cheap to buy. This is just as well because it is not at all an easy flower for the amateur to grow.

Freesia are not difficult to arrange. Oasis or Florapak is the most suitable support for the comparatively long and delicately curved slender stems. If a hole is made with a knitting needle or a small pointed cane in the required position, the placing of the thin stems is made much easier.

Drawing no. 46 shows an arrangement of freesia in an antique bronze goblet. The mechanics are a small block of Oasis covered with wire netting and strapped in position with Oasis adhesive tape. I like to use these because they ensure a much longer life to the Oasis. Water grasses and five variegated geranium leaves (*Pelargonium* 'Mrs. Henry Cox' or 'Marechal MacMahon') provide the necessary foliage interest and filling. The five geranium leaves are arranged

Oasis block covered
with wire netting
secured with Oasis tape

46 Arrangement of freesia, water grasses and decorative
geranium leaves in an antique bronze goblet. The rosette-like
flowers in the centre are 'Fantasy', a double variety of freesia

first so that they form a focal area, from and to which all
stems, grasses and flowers should emerge and converge. The
little rosette-like flowers in the centre are 'Fantasy', a
Parigo double variety of freesia.

I have done this arrangement a number of times. Sometimes I leave out the tallest pieces of water grass. Some prefer
it this way, others don't. What do you think?

28 Alstroemeria—and an Exercise in Error

Alstroemeria—the Peruvian lily—is long lasting and a very useful flower for the flower arranger. Particularly so are the Parigo hybrid varieties; they are large flowered and range in colour from delicate pink to a beautiful deep-toned 'old rose' red and from a clear yellow to orange. Used with their full length of stem—18 to 24 inches—they are ideal in large arrangements for churches or a hall, and cut to varying lengths they can be used equally well for medium-sized mass arrangements. They are never cheap, but if one considers the size of the bloom clusters, which are much larger than prize Chrysanthemum blooms, and the fact that there can be anything from six to twelve sizeable florets on one stem, and that all the buds will open, they are good value.

A small 7-inch high dolphin pedestal vase is an attractive container to use for a small or medium-sized arrangement where little base room is available, such as on an occasional table, bureau or mantelshelf (see drawings nos. 47 and 48, pages 121 and 123).

The aids or mechanics that are necessary for this type of arrangement are: a half block of Oasis about $4\frac{1}{2} \times 4\frac{1}{2}$ inches; some $1\frac{1}{2}$-inch or 2-inch mesh wire netting, cut to about 9 inches square; and some Oasis tape. Soak the block of Oasis well and then fit the wire netting in a domed fashion over it. Next, make absolutely sure that the outside of the pedestal cup is dry and strap down the dome of Oasis and wire netting with a length of Oasis tape. As I have said before, the tape will not adhere unless the outside of your container is perfectly dry. To make absolutely certain hold a lighted match or cigarette lighter near to the points of adhesion and then press the tape down firmly. It is then most unlikely that it will move, and the Oasis can be used time and time again until it disintegrates completely.

The flower requirements for this arrangement are three stems of alstroemeria and five pieces of foliage. I have used two stems of *Eucalyptus cinera* and three stems of *Eucalyptus globolus*. I could have used five pieces of either; alternatively, privet, cornus (dogwood), elaeagnus (wild olive) or any other foliage that has a graduated form of leaves on one stem. Beech or another similar foliage could also be used, but it must be remembered that any foliage that has small clusters of leaves on little branches growing on a main stem will give you a less stylised or more informal arrangement. Many people prefer this, and why not? Rhythmic proportions are the main essential. There are also many alternative flowers to alstroemeria that could be used in this arrangement: border carnations or scabious are two, long-stemmed sweet peas another.

Generally speaking, I find it best to start with one's planned outline. This ensures that the size proportions of the arrangement will be suited to the container and the location, and gives you a fair idea of the resultant silhouette. Further, not only will you be sure of a rhythmic placing of the larger units but you will also be certain that they each have a firm anchorage.

The longest piece of *Eucalyptus cinera*, which has a nice gentle curve (you can 'hand humour' it yourself if necessary), is cut to a length equal to about twice the height of the container and positioned centrally one-third from the back of the pedestal cup, slightly off vertical. Two pieces of

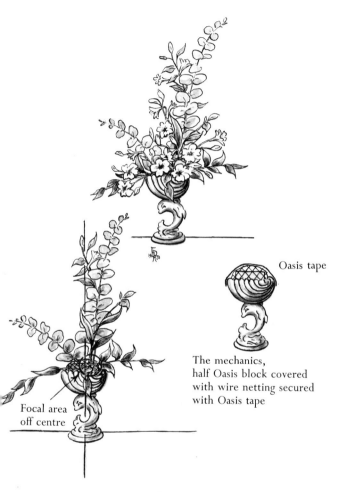

Oasis tape

The mechanics,
half Oasis block covered
with wire netting secured
with Oasis tape

Focal area
off centre

47 An exercise in error—unbalanced arrangement of alstroemeria and eucalyptus

Eucalyptus globolus are then fixed right and left, square with the frontal plane, as shown. A second piece of *Eucalyptus cinera* is then placed between the upright one and the left-hand horizontal, leaning slightly backwards. We have now established our outline and the focal point or area of origin.

From the three pieces of alstroemeria select one that has the best formation of buds and florets at the top. Strip all but two or three very carefully, as close as possible to the main stem, as you will have to use them all eventually. These little stems are very brittle, so I repeat—handle carefully. This long stripped stem is now positioned vertically, just behind the first piece of *Eucalyptus cinera*. The remaining stems of alstroemeria are now dealt with in exactly the same way and are positioned right and left, one leaning slightly forwards, the other slightly back.

To complete the arrangement position the remaining florets and buds which have been stripped and carefully put on one side. Be sure that *one* or *three* of the best of these have been selected for placing in the focal area. Finish off by covering any visible 'mechanics' with foliage, being sure to leave a small space at the back for topping up with water as required.

Subjects like alstroemeria that are very brittle are not always easy to insert into the Oasis, and I find a knitting needle, a pencil or a small pointed cane very useful for making holes in the Oasis for the fragile or whippy little stems.

Now, having spent all this time on the procedure, one should be able to stand back and admire the arrangement. But can we? Somehow it isn't really right. What is wrong with it?

The answer is very simple: we started wrong. The first placement, the tallest piece of *Eucalyptus cinera*, is both too

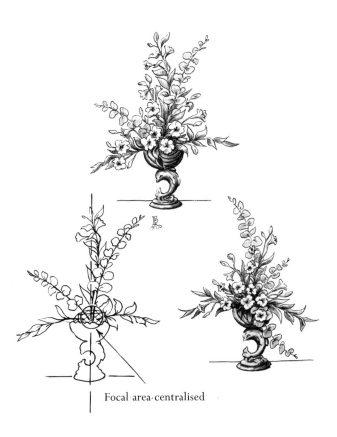

Focal area centralised

48   An exercise in error—two balanced arrangements of alstroemeria and eucalyptus

tall and placed off centre. From then onwards we were
working to a false focal area and consequently the arrangement appears to tilt backwards, accentuating the length of
the eucalyptus, which might otherwise have been acceptable.

The arrangements on page 123 (drawing no. 48), which
use the same quantities of the same flowers and foliage, have
centralised focal areas and are thus in balance.

29 Begonia

A half-hardy herbaceous plant, the begonia is a native of almost all the moist tropical countries; it is not, however, found in any part of Australasia, which has a flora and fauna all its own.

The begonia is extremely well known, both as a bedding plant and as a decorative house plant. I first became aware of its possibilities as a cut flower when a dog knocked off a whole plant at the root—my own fault because I hadn't sticked it. It was sad to see this lovely collection of four or five large blooms (it was one of those large, creamy, double-flowered varieties, I don't know the name) lying on the ground, but fortunately it was unbruised and unwilted. I put it in water, and before placing it in a sealing-wax-red Danish pottery vase (see drawing no. 49) I picked off one or two unwanted buds and leaves.

I have drawn it just as it appeared to me. It gave us much joy for the two or three days that it lasted.

The lop-sided, uneven leaves of the begonia, particularly of the *rex* varieties, are extremely useful to the flower arranger as a 'garnish' or a means of creating an accent in an arrangement. The colours and markings that are available, sometimes even on one plant, are quite amazing.

The begonia is a good house plant that, with care, will last for years. It prefers a good light, though away from direct sunlight. I think it is best watered through a base dish, any excess water being thrown away after half an hour's watering. Local humidity, essential if the plant is to do really well, can be provided by spraying around, but not directly onto, the leaves. Standing the plant in moist peat is equally effective.

49   Begonia is attractive as a cut flower, arranged here in a Danish pottery vase

Part 4—Bowl Gardens and Pots-et-fleurs

30 Bowl Gardens

Gold-fish bowls or large clear-glass brandy balloons make most attractive flower or plant containers, especially when used to simulate miniature gardens. These arrangements last particularly well in centrally-heated rooms because the flowers or plants are to a very considerable extent isolated from the excessively dry atmosphere so often prevalent with this type of heating.

The only aid you require for cut flowers is a small pin-holder secured with Oasis Fix. Very little water is needed— just enough to cover the top of the pinholder spikes. If necessary, conceal the 'mechanics' with pebbles or bun moss. Flowers and foliage must be well conditioned before arranging.

In drawing no. 50 I have shown two quite contrasting examples at B and C. In one I have used two orchids from an evening corsage. After wearing, it was floated for four or five hours in a bowl of water. The flowers completely recovered, so I dismantled it and, with the addition of two sprigs of bamboo foliage and a small spray of *Eucalyptus cinera*, I had an arrangement which lasted us a fortnight. We didn't get tired of it, largely I think because of the illusion of visual movement and aquatic life.

In the other I used two gladioli picked from the garden. Both had nearly finished blooming, having only a few buds and one or two flowers on each stem. One bud spike was placed centrally and upright, the other and a foliage spike at an angle opposite each other. Four, open, detached flowers

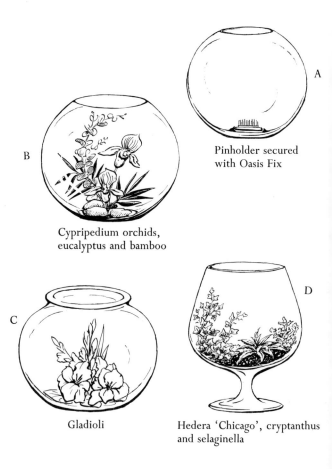

A

Pinholder secured
with Oasis Fix

B

Cypripedium orchids,
eucalyptus and bamboo

C

Gladioli

D

Hedera 'Chicago', cryptanthus
and selaginella

50   Examples of bowl gardens using cut flowers and plants

were grouped round these, completely hiding the pinholder. About three-quarters of an inch of water was added, and this arrangement lasted for six days.

If you want a bowl garden, this presents no difficulty. All you need is a depth of about 2 inches of a mixture of equal parts of sharp sand, peat and John Innes No. 3. Select suitable small plants, such as a miniature ivy (*Hedera helix* 'Chicago' or *H. h.* 'Glacier'), a selaginella and two small sedum. The small star-fish-like cryptanthus are most attractive in such arrangements (see drawing no. 50 D). Miniature ferns and *Tradescantia tricolour* are attractive too, but the latter grows so quickly that continual 'pinching off' will be necessary.

Start with your soil mixture just damp enough so that it will remain in a ball when squeezed in the hand. Very little, if any, watering will be required for quite a long time.

A good light is necessary, but avoid direct sunlight, for not only will a 'burning glass' effect be produced but also unsightly algae will form on the inside of the glass.

31 Pots-et-fleurs

This rather ugly name is generally used to describe arrangements of growing plants and cut flowers.

The possibilities are endless. Pots-et-fleurs can be elaborate—costly and exotic—or simple and really economical. In any case, to be able to use the same base for a number of different arrangements over a period is not only intriguing but, to my mind, also quite a challenge.

A simple dish garden is a good way to start. All you require are a shallow bowl or meat dish, some 'rocks' and pebbles, moss, a small jar and an Oasis bowl with a wire-netting-wrapped Oasis block.

Drawing no. 51 shows how you first arrange the Oasis bowl and the little jar. I like to anchor these with Oasis Fix or plasticine.

The *Asplenium nidus* (bird's nest fern) and tradescantia should be knocked out of their pots and placed in little cellophane bags. This enables individual control of watering.

All you have to do now is to group your plants and place the stones and moss around them so that the mechanics are hidden. Fill the spaces in between with moss and then arrange your cut flowers as you wish.

In drawing no. 51 I have shown two bulrushes, three guelder roses, two iris and three sprays of young beech or hazel. A small spray of camellia or laurel leaves gives weight to the base of the arrangement. In the little jars are lily of the valley and campanula—or any other small flower you like.

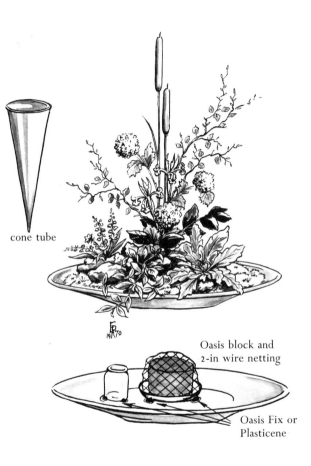

cone tube

Oasis block and
2-in wire netting

Oasis Fix or
Plasticene

51 Pot-et-fleur—a meat dish planted with an *Asplenium nidus* (bird's
    nest fern) and a tradescantia; the cut flowers and foliage com-
    prise iris, guelder roses, lily of the valley, campanula, bul-
    rushes, beech and camellia leaves

If the light is reasonable, this little dish garden will last for two or three weeks. After that, the plants should be re-potted and given a rest.

Permanent planted arrangements can be turned into pots-et-fleurs by using small metal cone tubes (obtainable from florists). These are pushed into the soil of the planted arrangement in the required position and then filled with water to take your cut flowers.

To create a change of focal point or a special attraction a small flowering plant—polyanthus, primrose or African violet—can be added somewhere in front. All you have to do is to make a hole and insert the pot. If the pot is too large, wrap the root in cellophane. Alternatively, a little posy of violets or wood anemones can be put into a small jar or a water-filled cellophane bag. As I have said, the possibilities are endless!

The pot-et-fleur shown on the cover of this book was specially designed for a modern open-plan house. In this case, the staircase rose almost centrally from one large multi-purpose room. The woodwork was mahogany colour and black. One wall had been stippled to give a flame effect. The remaining walls were of a soft beige with the faintest tint of orange. In a high gloss they not only helped lighting but also produced some most interesting and effective re-flections. The arrangement looked equally effective at the bottom of the open staircase or on the half-landing.

The container is a black plastic 'diablo' shaped garden planter in which have been planted (in John Innes No. 2) a cineraria, a polyanthus, an *Asplenium nidus* (bird's nest fern), a nephrolepis fern and a variegated ivy. Centrally, just be-hind the cineraria, has been positioned three-quarters of an Oasis brick, three sides of which are wrapped in plastic sheet to retain water. A pot or suitably-sized tin will do just as well. The point is to give the cut flowers a sufficiency of water without 'overwatering' the plants, which, given reasonable conditions, will thrive. The gladioli, or any other suitable cut flower, can be changed and changed again.

The planter I have used is 18 inches high with a bowl 12 inches in diameter and 5 inches deep, the gently sloping sides of which are ideal for plants, allowing a certain amount of aeration to the soil and thus to some extent overcoming the lack of drainage.

An arrangement of up to 48 inches high is well within the correct proportions. The advantages of such an arrangement are that it is quite portable, very stable and takes up little room.

A Basket Pot-et-fleur

With a little imagination there is almost no limit to what one can do with a few plants and flowers and an odd basket or bowl. And it need not necessarily be watertight! It is so easy to make a plastic lining to ensure that no damage is done to whatever it is you have decided to use and that no excess water spills and spoils furniture.

A hen basket makes an attractive container for plants, and so that one can have a bit more colour I have decided to use a few flowers as well—pot-et-fleur again (see drawing no. 52)!

First, line the inside of the basket with plastic sheeting (polythene bags can be used instead), sticking down the pleats with Sellotape and neatly cutting away any surplus round the edges. Then half fill the basket with moss (you can get this from florists) and position your plants as you want them in their pots. Pack moss tightly round each plant, covering the pots but leaving a little space round the stems

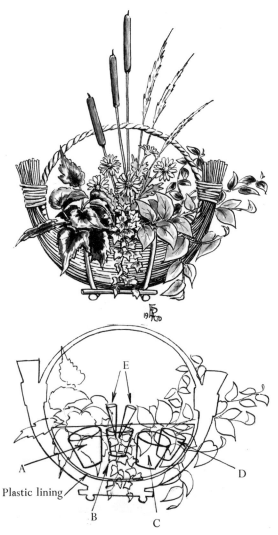

A

Plastic lining

B   C   D   E

52   Pot-et-fleur in a basket

to facilitate watering. Place the two cone tubes (E) either in the centre pot (B) or in any other position you want in the moss. Granulated peat can be used instead of moss.

Drawing no. 52 shows a *Begonia rex* (A), a variegated ivy (B), a scindapsus 'Marble Queen' or *Philodendron scandens* (sweetheart plant) (C) and a tradescantia (wandering Jew or wandering sailor) or zebrina (D). In the tubes (E) you can put any cut flowers you wish. I have used the single (daisy type) all-the-year-round chrysanthemums and three pieces of water grass or gardener's grass. Meadowsweet could be used if you like, or sorrel; there are countless meadow or hedgerow flowers available. The bulrushes I think give a little distinction to the arrangement, providing a design link with the strong colour and weight of texture of the begonias.

32 Plants Outside in Tubs

Plants in tubs, urns or other portable containers make an attractive feature of welcome at any front door. If the right selection is made, it is possible to have colour from early May until the arrival of the first frost. And not only is there a very wide range of colour available but one can have fragrance too. Furthermore, planting can be done at any time (in flower) up to the beginning of July.

Florists and garden centres offer a considerable range of jardinières, tubs, urns and stands in metal, plastic, timber and even concrete which can be used either separately or with hanging baskets. However, some people prefer to use more traditional or, conversely, unconventional containers —for instance, iron, brass or copper 'helmet' coal scuttles. There are many such bits of Victoriana that lend themselves to this use or that, with a little ingenuity, can be adapted so that the plants will happily live out their full cycle.

Drawing no. 53 shows a hand-thrown pottery 'egg crock' in which, years ago, we used to preserve eggs for the winter. It has two particular advantages: it occupies very little floor space and it raises the plants above the ground, thus making it easier to clean round as well as adding to the display.

The space above the little platform on the flower pot is lined with a polythene bag or plastic sheeting and then filled with a suitable compost—I prefer John Innes No. 2. I also pierce a few small holes in the bottom of the polythene bag to afford a limited amount of drainage in the event of accidental overwatering.

Wooden slats

Flower pot

53 An egg crock planted with geraniums, fuchsias, heliotrope, petunia, lobelia and a small-leafed variegated ivy

The selection of plants I have shown comprises geraniums, fuchsias, heliotrope (cherry pie), petunia, lobelia and a small-leafed variegated ivy. The heliotrope, as one of its names suggests, has a most attractive scent. Scented geranium and tobacco flower (nicotiana) are two more fragrant plants that can be used, as can many more rather exotic 'indoor' plants.

Part 5—High Summer and Autumn

33 The Crown of the Year

September, the crown of the year! And what a lovely month it generally is. Already those warm and sunny days are being followed by still, clear nights, and at any time now the mornings will be cool, crisp and even frosty. The grass is wet with heavy dews, and in the rose garden, still resplendent with the second flush of flowers, the bejewelled spider's web stretches from bush to bush. What a masterpiece of design this is. Now is the time when you should plan your roses for next year.

The dahlias, too, are still a mass of colour. Sad, isn't it, that any day now a sharp frost can reduce this brave show to a series of blackened columns, so why not cut the flowers and enjoy them while you may? You can afford to be extravagant, and while they last one mass arrangement after another can be the order of the day. Mix your colours! The red and yellow, purple and pink, orange and violet blooms, the pale green and russet foliage. Every colour and hue except blue is there. Julia Clements I think coined the phrase 'having fun with flowers'. The dahlia is one of the flowers that you can really have fun with and let yourself go. At this time of the year these flowers are cheap in the florists too.

The modern dahlia really is a first-class flower, both for mass show and for cutting. It lasts well as a cut flower, and its amazing range of colour is found in all varieties, from the smallest 'pom-pom' to the largest 'decorative' or 'cactus' types. It is tolerant of the most diverse conditions, and even the beginner, with a little thought and care, can produce flowers of a pretty high standard. If you haven't planted any, why not have some next year?

Colour plate 1 shows an arrangement of red, orange and gold dahlias ('David Howard', 'Chinese Lantern' and 'Carnival') in a fruit dish. A wire-netting-wrapped Oasis round comprises the mechanics, and this is secured to the dish with Oasis tape. This type of arrangement is particularly suitable for a desk or coffee table where space is at a premium.

If the rose is the 'Queen of Flowers', surely the chrysanthemum must be the 'King'. Like the rose, it has societies all its own, and whether grown in castle or cottage, in backyard greenhouse or acres of commercial glass houses it is all the same to the chrysanthemum. The amateur and the professional can compete on almost equal terms, for, given certain basic conditions, it is the 'know how' and practically twelve months' care that produces the results.

The name chrysanthemum derives from the Greek *chrysos* meaning 'gold' and *anthos* meaning 'flower'. Our greenhouse and early-flowering chrysanthemums have been developed from *C. indicum* and *C. morifolium* (syn. *C. sinense*) found originally in China and Japan, where they have been cultivated as a national flower for thousands of years.

As a cut flower the chrysanthemum is a paradox, for while being one of the longest lasting in water of any large flower it is, at the same time, the most brittle. Under ideal conditions and with the right treatment, it will last a fortnight to three weeks; given the wrong treatment, it will last only a few hours.

The construction of the flower is interesting. On average, there are 400 to 500 petals in a $3\frac{1}{2}$-inch to 4-inch bloom, and these are crammed into a calyx of only $\frac{3}{4}$-inch diameter. The point of contact of each little petal is less than a pin's head. One petal more or less holds another in position, and the slightest knock, loosening two or three petals, will cause almost all the remainder eventually to drop off from the calyx. By the same token, bruised petals can be removed if gently pulled *at right angles* away from the centre. This is called 'dressing', and a certain amount is permitted at chrysanthemum shows.

A bloom that has been severely knocked and has 'dropping' petals need not be thrown away. All that is necessary is to locate the place where the damage has been done and to drop molten candle wax into this area. This will seal off the damaged part and the bloom will then last its normal life in water.

Chrysanthemums must be properly conditioned before arranging if they are to stand up to the unfavourable conditions found in the modern centrally-heated home. The average reputable florist will normally have done this before sale ; that is, the chrysanthemums will have been stood in deep water in a cool place for at least six hours, about 2 inches of the bottom of the stems having been crushed. Even so, I think it wise to resist the temptation to arrange a gift of chrysanthemums immediately. There is bound to be a slight wilting in transit from the shop to your home. This transpiration—loss of moisture content—can so easily be replaced by giving them *at least an hour's good, deep, cool drink.* Most florists attach to the wrapping a 'care' card, which gives detailed instructions. This card is compulsory with all Interflora orders, and its instructions are well worth reading and following.

There are a large number of chrysanthemums that the amateur can grow in a small garden, the size of bloom obtainable depending on the amount of disbudding that is done. It is preferable that the plants are dug up after flowering and protected from severe winter frosts. They should be watched carefully so as not to be allowed to dry up. In the spring, generally in March, new shoots appear. The plants should then be placed in the light, and cuttings should be taken from the shoots when they are about 3 inches long. If only a few plants are required, the simplest thing to do is to divide the clump and plant out. Chrysanthemums are hungry plants, and require a rich and nourishing soil.

The potted chrysanthemum which is such a popular gift these days need not be thrown away after flowering. If planted out they will generally survive. It is, however, unlikely that the dwarf habit will be retained; this has been artificially induced at the nursery.

Drawing no. 54 on page 147 illustrates an attractive and economical way of arranging a few chrysanthemums. It comprises five large incurve yellow blooms, some preserved oak of a donkey-brown hue, five dyed purple stems of bearded barley and seven small purple asters (inset). The Japanese pottery vase was of a greyish cream glaze.

Michaelmas daisies, achillea and, of course, coreopsis, helianthus and heliopsis, and even some of the asters, are still at their colourful best in the herbaceous borders. Now you must give a thought to how you will arrange that border for next year. Whether you believe in good, deep digging or surface tilling, now is the time when you must seriously think about routing out and separating, fertilising and putting humus back into the soil. Now is the time when you will value that compost heap.

And while you are planning give a thought to next year's cutting for the house. Planting in groups—with, of course, the tallest subjects at the back—will give you the best of both worlds. The flowers you cut for the house will hardly be missed because there is no symmetry to be interfered

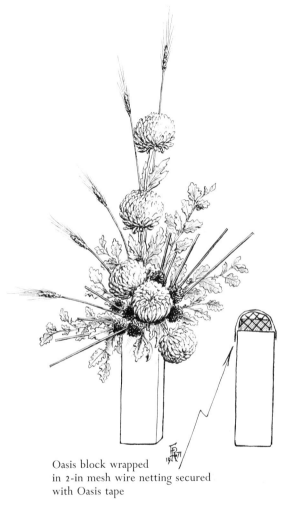

Oasis block wrapped
in 2-in mesh wire netting secured
with Oasis tape

54 Five incurve chrysanthemums arranged with preserved oak,
dyed bearded barley and asters in a Japanese pottery vase

with. Another advantage of this type of planting (planned well ahead) is that you can fill the empty spaces left when the daffodils, tulips, hyacinths, wallflowers and suchlike are finished with some of the large variety of bedding annuals that are available. Many of these are now good flowers for cutting.

If you really think about it, you can have colour for cutting and spectacle in that herbaceous border from March until October, and with the careful positioning of a few shrubs and small trees, such as acers, sumacs and berberis, you can have some colour all the year round.

34 Making the Most of Spray Chrysanthemums

The advent of the American spray, all-the-year-round chrysanthemum has widened the scope of the flower arranger more than any other flower introduced since the War. Very few people dislike it, unlike the 'bloom', and it is equally long lasting but tougher than the 'bloom'. It has a wide range of colour and form; there are single-, double- and anemone-centred varieties, and even 'Tokyo' and 'Rayonnante' which are spider-like in form. The stems are strong without being bulky, and the foliage is in proportion and decorative. American spray chrysanthemum is most economical too, because by carefully 'cutting out' the little flowers you can obtain long, medium and short stems—the long and medium stems for your outline, the short for filling and sometimes some to spare.

Drawing no. 55 shows how an arrangement up to 2½ feet high can be made with four stems of American spray chrysanthemums and five carnations. The foliage I have used is beech, but any other in season will be equally appropriate. For instance, in summer, corn and grasses make a delightful combination with 'Bonnie Jean', the white single variety that is so like the marguerite daisy but has the advantage that it lasts four or five times as long as this flower which typifies the countryside in summer.

I think my drawing is self-explanatory, except for the little arrangement in the brandy balloon. If you count up you will find that this is composed of the seven to ten spares you can be left with if you are careful with your placing. The foliage I have used in this case is a small-leafed oak.

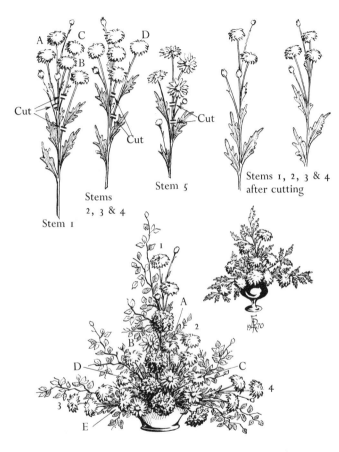

Arrangement of four stems of American spray chrysanthemums, carnations and beech. The little arrangement in the brandy balloon is composed of the spare chrysanthemums left over from the main arrangement; the foliage is a small-leafed oak

35 Green—a Colour for All Seasons

I wonder, do we always appreciate the value of green? The variety of tones and shades in this colour is infinite. Foliage of some sort is available all the year round, and almost every kind of leafage will last well in water, provided that conditioning has been attended to before arranging.

Conditioning is largely a matter of common sense and experience. Foliage with hard, woody stems should be split or crushed for about 3 inches at the bottom. Beech, oak, larch and laurel are obvious examples. Total immersion is advised for subjects like arum leaves, hosta, artichoke, helleborus and bergenia that have a large fleshy area. Privet, myrtle, forsythia, eucalyptus and various berberis require little conditioning. Vine, ivy, wild clematis and a host of ferns are also available. And we must not forget *Senecio greyi*, *Elaeagnus macrophylla* and *E. ebbingii*, the foliage of which is silver-grey on the reverse side. The list is endless.

Drawing no. 56 shows an all-green foliage arrangement in a copper pedestal urn. Note the mechanics used with this large container; they dispense with a deal of useless space, at the same time providing a secure anchorage for the long and somewhat heavy subjects. I have used wild angelica, Solomon's seal, artichoke, variegated ivy, young larch bearing green cones, hosta and green poppy seed heads.

This cool and impressive arrangement is very easy to do. Start with the three tallest angelica; then place the artichokes, followed by the Solomon's seal, one leaning slightly forwards and the other slightly back. The same applies to the larch. Next arrange your hosta leaves, and then the

poppy seed heads, leaving the largest of these and the ivy for
your focal point.

Later in the year many of the foliages available will have
turned to their beautiful autumn colourings. Be sure you
gather what you want before they begin to drop. And don't
be too late in gathering what you need for preserving.

Oasis wrapped in 1½-in or 2-in wire netting

Plastic lining

False bottom on flower pot

56   Foliage arrangement in an antique copper urn

Part 6—Party Flowers, and Fruit and Flowers

36 Party Flowers—the Buffet Table

There are so many other important things to be considered when giving a party that the flowers are often left until the last moment, and then unnecessary expense is incurred and the result is often far from satisfactory.

There are many ways of arranging flowers for a party. The buffet, dining table or bar are focal points that can look very unsightly immediately the food, glass, cutlery and napery are disturbed. Planned arrangements of flowers, however, will ensure a reasonably attractive appearance for the whole of the party.

As with everything else, it pays to plan, and every arrangement should be practical as well as decorative. None should interfere with the picking up or putting down of plates, dishes, glasses and cutlery. They should occupy as little base space as possible, and tall arrangements particu- · larly should have good firm bases so that there is no danger of their being knocked over.

One very simple method of decorating a buffet table is to use wine or champagne bottles and coloured candles clustered with small flowers, as shown in drawing no. 57. Between these, spaced at suitable intervals, are placed small arrangements in little bowls or Oasis cups—again, each with a coloured candle. And all the arrangements are linked together with ivy or some other creeper trails.

First, fill the wine or champagne bottle with water; this will ensure a reasonable stability. Next, insert the candle cup in the bottle, securing it with Oasis Fix; place the Oasis block in the cup and then push the candle through to the recess specially made for it in the bottom of the cup. Be sure

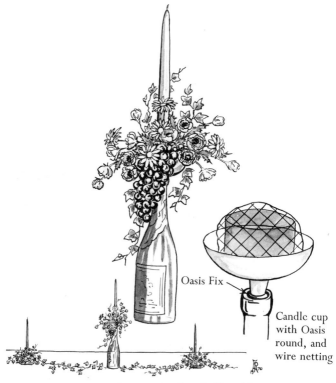

Oasis Fix

Candle cup
with Oasis
round, and
wire netting

57   A suggestion for a buffet table

to burn the bottom of the candle with a match or lighter to seal the end; if you don't, there is every likelihood that the wick will soak up water from the Oasis block, in which case the candle will never light. Now place a dome of 1½-inch to 2-inch mesh wire netting over the candle down onto the 'Oasis' block, and all is ready for the flowers.

I have used mixed coloured ranunculus, all-the-year-round American spray chrysanthemums ('Tuneful'—a lovely golden brown colour), variegated ivy trails and artificial grapes. Normally, I do not like using artificial materials, but these grapes are so beautifully made, realistic and light in weight that they have a definite artistic as well as a practical merit. They are washable, available in black and green, and can be purchased from florists.

The same materials (except for the grapes) are used in the little intermediate arrangements in the Oasis cups. When you have established the relative positions of the arrangements, place the connecting ivy trails with each end under an arrangement, and be sure to pin them down to the table cloth at frequent intervals.

37 Fruit and Flowers

A very wide field of shape and colour harmony is open to the flower arranger who uses fruit and flowers together. Pineapple leaves with their bluish grey-green and powdered texture link perfectly with the bloom on grapes. The polished cheeks of apples provide a colour harmony with the numerous citrus fruits available. Plums and tomatoes, peaches and pears, and the ubiquitous banana all have different and most exciting textures, shapes and colours which combine perfectly with flowers.

Any largish dish or basket, with an Oasis bowl for the flowers, is a suitable container. Drawing no. 58 shows two flat raffia baskets. The vertical one is supported by a suitably bent strip of flat metal or a wedge-shaped block of wood. Soft wire or nails are used to secure the basket to the supports. The Oasis bowl or other container can, if necessary, be stuck with Oasis Fix or wired to the basket.

For my arrangement I have used three large gladioli, six leaves and two loops, some vine leaves and three or four geums from the garden. The bright red of the geums make a delightful analagous colour harmony with the clear yellow of the 'American Express' gladioli and the various fruits.

The pineapple, which provides the focal point, is placed centrally, leaning slightly forwards. Round this and right up to the Oasis bowl (hiding the mechanics) dried bun moss is arranged to form a cushion-like base for the other fruits. A great variety of these cushion-like woodland mosses can be had for the gathering; most of them dry easily and retain much of their original colour. If the moss is carefully and artistically arranged, subsequent removal of the fruit for consumption will not ruin the effect of the arrangement.

By the way, did you know that pineapple tops can be

Wood
Wedge

Oasis bowl and wire mesh

58   Basket arrangement of 'American Express' gladioli, geums, vine leaves, a pineapple, grapes and various other fruits

planted in a pot of cactus soil and that a quite decorative house plant will result?

A bowl of fruit on a table not only provides colour but also seems to create a feeling of well being. Add flowers to this and you have comparative luxury. This need not be expensive—in fact, with a little thought, quite the reverse.

Oasis
Fix

59   Arrangement of fruit and flowers in a pedestal dish with a
candle. The flowers and foliage used are Michaelmas daisies, rose
buds, American spray chrysanthemums, fern and wild clematis
(old man's beard)

A pedestal cake or fruit dish and a small candlestick with a candlecup and candle are all you require to create a table-centre that is both attractive and economical. Instead of a pedestal cake or fruit dish, a large dinner plate could, of course, be used. However, the pedestal dish, in raising the fruit a few inches, adds considerably to the attractiveness of the whole arrangement and has the advantage of taking up much less table room.

The choice of flowers and foliage you can use is very wide indeed. Berries, dried seed heads, ferns, grasses, autumn leaves and old man's beard (wild clematis) can be found well into the winter. Michaelmas daisies, the odd rosebud (opened indoors) and one stem of American spray chrysanthemum are quite sufficient flowers to make an attractive arrangement to crown the colour of the fruit. The arrangement illustrated in drawing no. 59 is composed of just these flowers, with one or two pieces of fern and old man's beard.

If you are in doubt about using real grapes, artificial ones are available. They are inexpensive and, as I have said before, almost indistinguishable from the real thing. Real grapes have one great disadvantage: they split so easily and the juice causes premature rotting, affecting the other fruit in the bowl.

Oasis Fix may not be necessary at the base of the candlestick if the dish has a reasonably flat inside. Don't forget to seal the candle by melting the wax at the bottom end.

Part 7—Contemporary and Dried
Flower Arrangements; Feathers

Many people are of the opinion that massed or massed-line arrangements are out of keeping with modern or contemporary décor, and while I do not entirely agree with this I do think that a great deal of care and attention to detail is necessary however you decide to use flowers in such settings.

Those 'containers'—vases, bowls, pots, jugs—which among traditional and period furnishings cry out for flowers are difficult, if not impossible, to fit into the somewhat stark, slick, efficient bareness of many present-day living rooms. Beautifully proportioned pieces of contemporary potting, however, such as bowls and ash trays which are designed primarily to be functional, relying on sheer clarity of line and proportions for their decorative appeal, are ideal for flower arrangements in modern rooms.

Such a piece of modern potting is the matt white block ash tray shown in drawing no. 60. It is about $5\frac{1}{2} \times 5\frac{1}{2} \times 2$ inches. In the top is a sunken circular recess which has been glazed (matt) a beautiful deep mushroom-brown. This recess is deep enough to take a medium-sized pinholder.

The five bulrushes in my arrangement (drawing no. 60) carry on the colour of the bowl, and the curled purply brown and soft deep green, rose-pink-streaked leaf of the *Cordyline terminalis* (or *Dracaena terminalis* known as 'Dragon Plant') provides a perfect colour link with the pink water lily. The two dried rush leaves give balance to the bulrushes.

The pinholder is secured with Oasis Fix, as shown, and

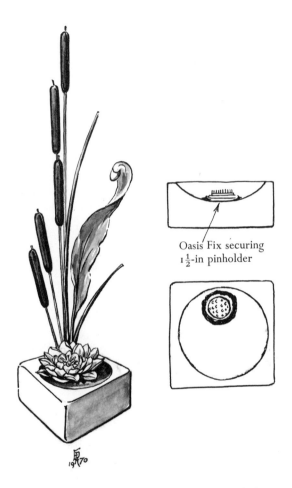

Oasis Fix securing
$1\frac{1}{2}$-in pinholder

60   Arrangement of five bulrushes, two dried rush leaves, a
     cordyline leaf and a water lily in a square ash tray

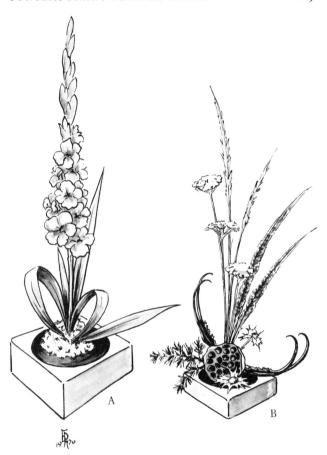

61 Two other arrangements suitable for this square ash tray.
A consists of a single gladioli with a pair of leaves and leaf bows;
B is composed of two stems of water grass, three stems of
achillea, two pheasant feathers, dried pine and sea holly, two
South African vogel pods and a lotus seed head

the bulrushes, after having been cut to the required length, should have their ends sealed with Gutter Percha tape (obtainable from florists) and then be waxed. This prevents rotting and, provided that their heads have been varnished to prevent seeding, the bulrushes will be almost everlasting.

Water lilies tend to open and close at sunrise and sunset. To prevent this little beads of molten candle wax should be carefully dropped into the centre of the flower.

Cordyline and dracaena leaves can be curled with gentle 'hand humouring'. As alternatives to these there are many dried materials available, such as aspidistra, loquat, etc. These, however, lack the beautiful variation found in the cordyline and dracaena foliage.

Another 'contemporary' arrangement suitable for this container is shown in drawing no. 61 A. It consists of one perfect gladioli spike with a pair of leaves and leaf bows; bun moss hides the mechanics.

The dried arrangement on the same page (drawing no. 61 B) consists of two stems of water grass, three stems of achillea, two pheasant feathers, dried pine and sea holly. The two curled South African vogel pods accentuate the focal point, which is a lotus seed head.

Both these arrangements are placed in a medium-sized pinholder secured with Oasis Fix.

39 A Problem of Shape

To the flower arranger a container is anything that will hold
water. A few containers may have been designed specifically
for flowers, but the majority, it would seem, have no purpose
at all other than as ornaments. Many, particularly those of
pottery, are in themselves of extremely good design but
in shapes that do not seem suitable for flowers.

The rectangular piece of Danish pottery shown in drawing
no. 62 is a case in point. It is approximately $7\frac{1}{2} \times 5\frac{1}{2} \times$
$2\frac{1}{2}$ inches. It is glazed in an attractive and subtle combination
blue, white and brown. The lack of depth from front to
back makes this appear at first sight to be a difficult subject
for flower arranging, since any conventional fan or triangular
arrangement would not only be flat and unbalanced but
also lack unity and rhythm. However, the almost square
proportions of this piece of pottery are to my mind most
attractive and any flower arrangement in it should not
interfere in any way with these. I have therefore created an
illusion of visual movement and rhythm around the container which has produced a sense of depth and has made
possible the very simple central positioning of the three
stems of hydrangea and the three bulrushes. The squareness
of the container thus provides a stable base and a visual
anchorage for the seeming movement of the rest of the
arrangement.

The mechanics for such an arrangement are very simple—
just a $2\frac{1}{2}$-inch or 3-inch rectangular pinholder, on top of

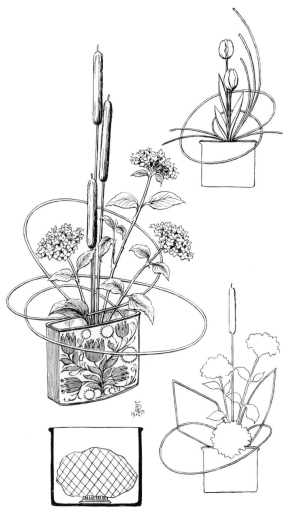

62   A problem of shape—three solutions

which is placed crumpled wire netting. If you wish you can secure the pinholder with Oasis Fix.

Instead of basketry cane, as I have used, loops can be made of stripped wistaria or any other long, straight twigs.

My two thumbnail sketches show alternative arrangements suitable for this container. Tulips, chrysanthemums or dahlias could be used instead of hydrangea—and tulips are perhaps the most obviously suitable flower. But I have emphasised hydrangea for two reasons. First, because they are available in a wide range of colour and, secondly, because they provide a very cheap means for experimentation and practice.

To return to the illusion of visual movement and rhythm. The upper one of my two thumbnail sketches is a particular case in point. By themselves, the two tulips would appear quite static, but the whorl of basketry cane, together with the three curved ascending stems rising from the three horizontal ones, seems to put 'life' into the arrangement.

40 Dried Arrangements

Dried arrangements should not be confused with artificial or so-called 'everlasting' flower arrangements. In my opinion these are mostly inanimate, synthetic dust-collectors.

As part of the Christmas scene, finishing with Twelfth Night, artificial flowers, ferns, leaves and holly have their place. Many are very realistic, and they have one great advantage in that they are quite unaffected by central heating, which at this time of the year is on full blast. Some of the wax or plastic Christmas roses and the larger poinsettia, for instance, can be used as focal points in real or dried flower arrangements.

An example of this is shown in colour plate 2. The large plastic poinsettia and the bright red ribbon bows seem quite in keeping with the real holly, sitka spruce, *Eucalyptus cinera*, various cones and large teazles—largely I think because of the choice of container. This is a large goldfish bowl, in the centre of which has been placed a 'kilner' jar surrounded by a variety of coloured glass baubles —another effective way of concealing the arranger's mechanics.

To return to dried arrangements as such. Some of us prefer to use dry Oasis as a fixing base, while others use one of the various polystyrene or other plastic substances obtainable from all good florists. Oasis is much easier to use but is not quite so permanent. When using Oasis, be sure to wrap it in a suitable mesh wire netting if large and heavy materials are to be arranged. Kitchen foil is a satisfactory

63   An easy-to-make winter-time arrangement

wrapping for Oasis if light-weight materials are used. With polystyrene or any of the other plastic foam blocks, I advise a little Oasis Fix at the ends of the stems of long and heavy subjects. This will satisfactorily prevent movement, which eventually causes considerable disintegration of the polystyrene at the point where the stems enter it, and is a very necessary precaution if the arrangement is to be wrapped and packed away for future use.

In a mixed arrangement of fresh and dried flowers, the stems of the latter (unless they are mounted on wires) should be protected from rotting, which can be caused by the water or wet Oasis and Florapak. There are various ways of protecting stems: waxing, varnishing and taping. Personally, I prefer to tape and then varnish.

The choice of dried flower and foliage materials available to the flower arranger is ever increasing. Recently, a wide variety of 'composite' flowers has become available. These are cleverly built up from husks, calyces, seeds and buds to represent flowers. Some are mounted on natural stems and others on wires, and some you will have to mount yourself. A number are in natural colours, and others have been bleached and dyed. A few of the colours are garish and, to my way of thinking, even vulgar, but careful selection will produce a mixture such as that shown in colour plate 3. This arrangement is in a 12-inch high pottery jar decorated with a beautiful leaf design in muted greens and dusty gold, blending well with the golden pheasant feathers, bulrushes, focal artichoke and all the other components of this 3-foot high arrangement.

Striking a much more sophisticated note is the arrangement shown in colour plate 4. This is simply two golden bulrushes, sea fern, coral and fungi in a shallow three-legged bowl. At the base of this arrangement are some

64 Dried arrangement in an upturned kidney-shaped bowl

large flint pebbles and a lump of blue rock quartz. These conceal the mechanics, which is a large pinholder (3 inches in diameter), and provide a complementary colour harmony and the necessary weight at the base. The little ivory figurine seems to complement this arrangement—perhaps providing a tranquil but live link with the dead.

The little arrangement, just over 12 inches high, shown in illustration no. 63 on page 173 is an example of one of the many permutations of such easy-to-make winter-time arrangements. Eight or nine units are sufficient, with some preserved beech or oak and some dried bracken or fern. This arrangement is composed of nine units. They are three pencil bulrushes, one poppy head, one acacia flower, two Mexican wood lilies and two zepheri flowers, the lower one providing the focal point. There are countless other dried materials that can be used.

If you want a little Christmassy arrangement, substitute holly for the beech and Christmas roses (*Helleborus niger*) for the acacia and zepheri flowers, and spray the whole with 'snow' and a little glitter.

Physalis (Cape gooseberry or Chinese lantern) is one of the few natural brightly coloured dried flowers; it is quite easy to grow and dry too. I have used these in the arrangement shown in illustration no. 64 on page 175 with shiny mahogany-brown loquat leaves, three tan 'Sidney' roses, two sulphur-yellow bulrushes, some duum spikes and outline leaves made from basketry cane. The container is of particular interest. It consists of an Oasis bowl (a saucer or sugar bowl can be used instead) stuck onto the base of an upturned kidney-shaped, mahogany-brown bulb bowl with Oasis Fix; the Oasis bowl is painted brown to match the bulb bowl. The advantage of this is that not only is a stable base provided but also the whole arrangement is raised, thus

Styrofoam block held by
Oasis adhesive tape

65 Arrangements of dried materials in a china tube and a narrow-
necked bottle vase

Styrofoam block stuck to pan

66   Arrangement of dried materials in a copper pan

showing the beauty of the loquat leaves to better advantage.

The arrangements and their mechanics shown in drawings nos. 65 and 66 on pages 177 and 178 are further examples of the scope of dried flower arrangement. Feathers, cone-bearing larch twigs, dried Jerusalem or Chinese artichokes, grasses, dried maidenhair fern and achillea (yarrow or milfoil) are but a few of the enormous choice of materials available.

41 Feathers

Two of the most beautiful feathers I know are peacock and pheasant. Both have a colour and rhythm that, I think, is unequalled in any other. The colours in the former are positively jewel-like. Such a pity that some people think them unlucky.

I did a little research into this superstition and found that it, like so many others, is based on sound common sense— that is, common sense from the point of view of certain 'interested' parties. In medieval days the peacock, like the swan in this country, was a royal bird. What could be more natural therefore than that the priesthood should proclaim to all and sundry that bad luck, hell and damnation would befall anyone who should kill and eat one. Peacocks, I understand, are actually good eating, as are swans. (The latter, I am told, like some water fowl, should be skinned before cooking.) Anyway, I for one simply cannot believe that anything so beautiful should be unlucky.

Ostrich and marabou are two other feathers available that could be used—but I feel strongly, with the greatest possible restraint.

The large arrangement in an antique bronze cherub pedestal fruit bowl shown in illustration no. 67 should be displayed in a large room or on a half-landing. It looks particularly attractive standing on a Victorian walnut or mahogany aspidistra stand. Black and green artificial grapes provide the focal area, from which all the feathers radiate.

For smaller situations an arrangement such as the smaller

67 Two arrangements using feathers. The larger one in the
cherub pedestal vase is simply composed of peacock feathers and
artificial grapes. The smaller one consists of five peacock
feathers, five dried acacia flowers and five glass baubles mounted
on taped florists' wire

one shown in illustration no. 67 is more suitable. Five peacock feathers, five dried acacia flowers are arranged in the square Japanese-style dull green glazed vase. Five blue glass baubles have been mounted on heavy taped (brown) florists' wire; these pick up the iridescent blue in the peacock feathers. The centre one, slightly recessed, provides the focal point in this arrangement.

———————

If you have enjoyed reading this book as much as I have writing and illustrating it, our time will have been well spent. Remember that all the arrangements I have described first appeared in my mind's eye. A similar exercise of your imagination will, I am sure, help you to achieve increasingly more successful arrangements of flowers.